CHIC HOME INTERIORS

LINKS

CHIC HOME INTERIORS

Edition 2014

Author: Carles Broto

Graphic design & production: Roberto Bottura & Oriol Vallès

Collaborator: Clara Sola y Jacobo Krauel

Cover design: Oriol Vallès, graphic designer

Collaborator: Text: Contributed by the architects, edited by Naomi Ferguson

© LinksBooks

Jonqueres, 10, 1-5

08003 Barcelona, Spain

Tel.: +34-93-301-21-99

info@linksbooks.net

www.linksbooks.net

CHIC HOME INTERIORS

LINKS

INDEX

INTRODUCTION

Creativity and invention are dependent on space and the possibilities afforded by it. Architectural work in small spaces is often a challenge to achieve the seemingly impossible: to turn a small area into a comfortable dwelling in which the lack of living space is not perceived. Great architectural works are not necessarily those that are measured by the number of square meters, but those which use every square meter to its best potential.

The aim of this book is to display designs, realized with outstanding skill, that create stimulating environments in small spaces. This is a complicated task that is not limited to removing partitions, building mezzanines and incorporating specific furniture for the needs of the space. A skillful use of a small space requires far more: a focus on the particular requirements and comfort of the clients, and an aesthetic design in which the architecture adapts elegantly to the restrictions of a limited floor area.

These works show the imaginative force of the designs in which small premises can be transformed into comfortable dwellings, regardless of their original use or location.

The designs include apartments created after the division of a large flat, small single-family dwellings in the country and fantasy terrace dwellings. They are complemented by plans and explanations of the architectural work carried out in each scheme, detailing the creative process.

i29 Interior Architects

Home 07

Amsterdam, the Netherlands

Photographs: contributed by i29 Interior Architects

This family apartment for four people is situated in a stately building in southern Amsterdam, Holland. The original structure, with rooms for staff, a double hall and long hallways with lots of doors has been transformed into a spacious, transparent dwelling full of light and air. Design features such as abstract cutout patterns, give the residence a distinctive identity.

A kitchen in combination with floor to ceiling cabinets has laser-cut front panels, all spray-painted white. This pattern results in a dynamic mixture of open and closed cabinets, the holes also function as integrated handgrips. The transparency of the object's skin gives depth to the volume, which is complimented by furniture such as the Grcic chair one. An atrium with open staircases brings natural light from a large roof light into the living area.

Along the open staircase a pine-clad two story high wall connects the two levels. Upstairs, the master bedroom is situated next to a large bathroom finished with Patricia Urquiola tiles, glass, and wooden cabinets. The designers at i29, Jasper Jansen and Jeroen Dellensen, aim to create intelligent design with striking images. With a keen eye for detail, the team attempts to get at the core of things, equipping their interiors with just the right touch of unique features to bring out the essence of the surrounding space. The clarity and simplicity of their design language has caught the eye of numerous juries and resulted in several design prizes.

Architecture:
i29 Interior Architects

Contractor:
Smart Interiors

Interior construction:
Kooijmans Interiors

Materials:
Pinewood, white epoxy flooring

Furniture:
Chair one, Magis Constantin Grcic /
Loop stand table, Hay / GloBall lights,
Jasper Morrison, Flos /
Custom made kitchen & cabinets

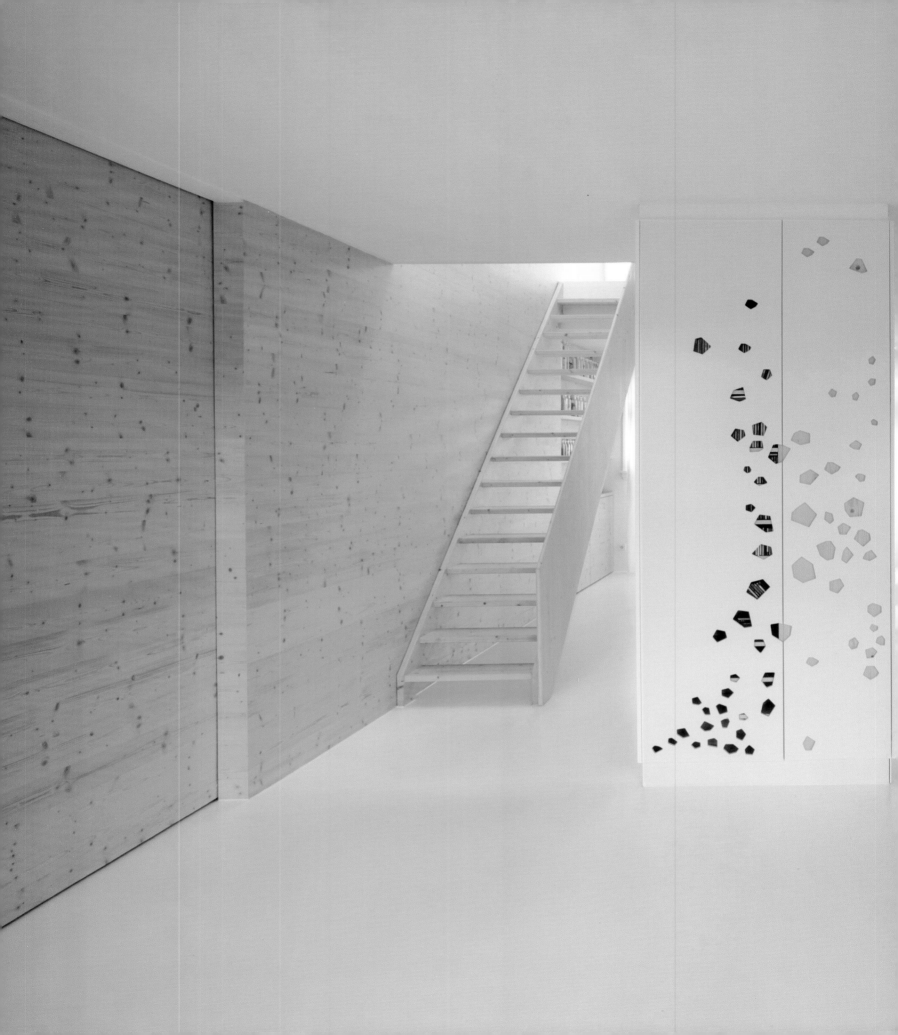

Design features such as abstract cutout patterns give the residence a distinctive identity.

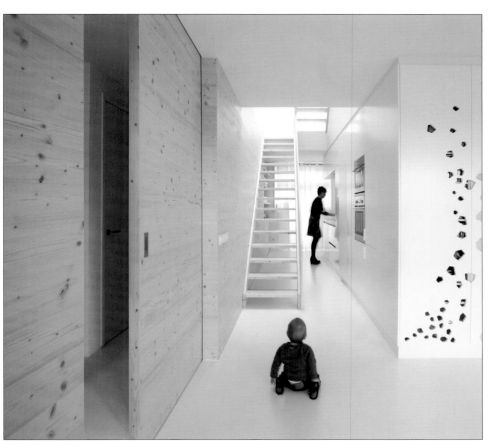

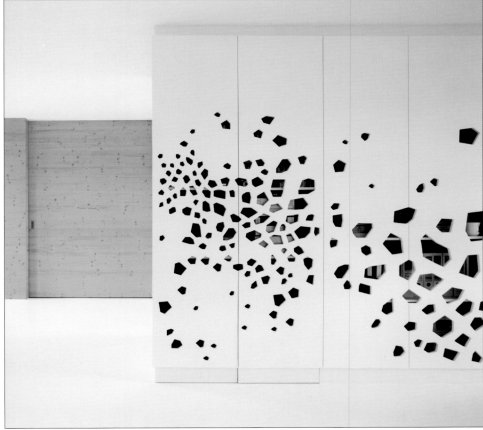

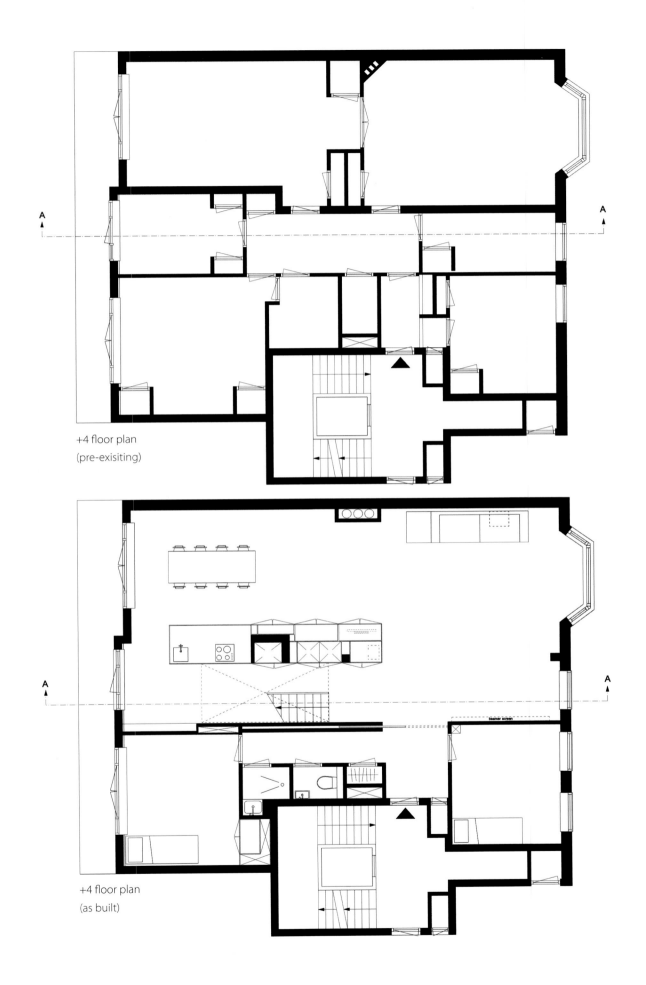

+4 floor plan
(pre-exisiting)

+4 floor plan
(as built)

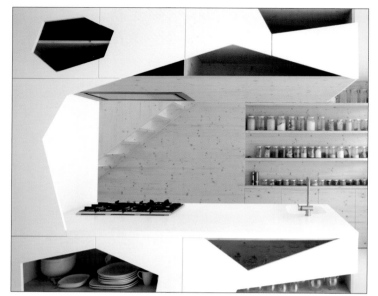

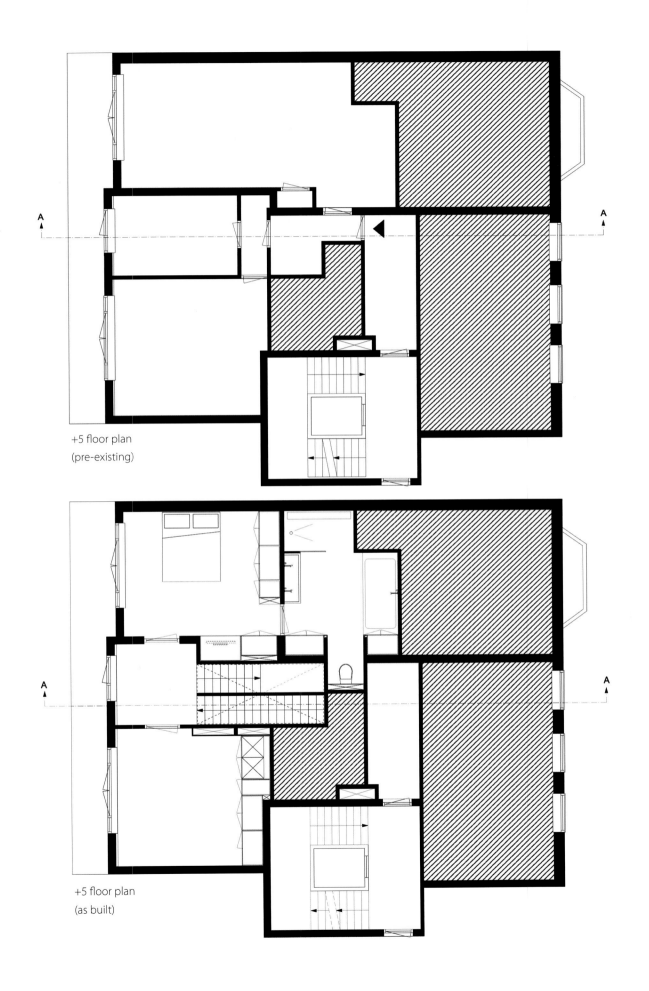

+5 floor plan
(pre-existing)

+5 floor plan
(as built)

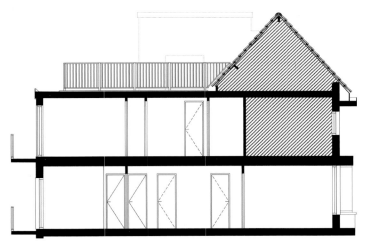
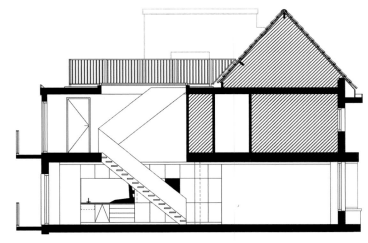

Cross section (pre-exisiting)

Cross section (as built)

Stefan Antoni Olmesdahl Truen Architects (SAOTA)

COVE 6

Pezula Golf Estate, Knysna, South Africa

Photographs: Stefan Antoni

The aim of this project was to design a house inspired by its indigenous fynbos surroundings. The property is part of the recently established private estate known as The Cove. The site, located on an exposed cliff edge overlooking a rocky peninsula, is perched above a dramatic seascape with spectacular views, and is one of six exclusive use areas permitted on this reserve. The clients, a well-traveled couple from the UK, wanted a house with seamless indoor-outdoor living for summer holiday retreats. The house had to take maximum advantage of the spectacular views and surrounding landscape.

The site is situated in a unique environment whose natural attributes required careful consideration, with particular regard to the sensitivity of its location on the southern coast of the East Head at Knysna. It is characterized by its rolling landforms and the highly varied, dense indigenous vegetation.

The architects opted for materials that would complement the natural color pallet and textures of the site thus minimizing the impact both during construction and after completion. The result is a pavilion that blends with and does not overpower nature, with a cohesive architectural character in terms of scale, proportion and the articulation of the building form. It is airy, yet firmly anchored into the landscape by means of heavy, stone clad walls.

Externally, fynbos plantings provided the feeling that the house is set in nature and does not disturb the natural beauty. The building fits comfortably into the natural contours of the orientation of the site. Cantilevered structures such as the pool and elevated timber decks where allowed to protrude beyond the building lines and to allow indigenous vegetation to grow below.

The location of the site invited large glazed areas and extensive use of outdoor spaces, with each aspect of the house having a private terrace or deck. The open plan linear composition of the interior spaces allows views from every room. To take advantage of the sea and surrounding golf course views and to provide protection from the area's extreme coastal climate, the living spaces were designed with southwest/northeast orientations, resulting in an open flowing space with both uninterrupted sea-facing terraces and protected courtyards. The main living spaces form the link between inside and outside. The orientation gives the owners the option of sheltered courtyards on the leeward side in poor weather conditions or the use of extensive terraces on the windward side on sunny and wind free days. The through-views also ensure that one always experiences the sea and adjacent rolling landscapes.

Architecture:
Stefan Antoni, Greg Truen,
Johann van der Merwe
Structural engineer:
Kanty & Templer
Contractor:
Cape Island Homes

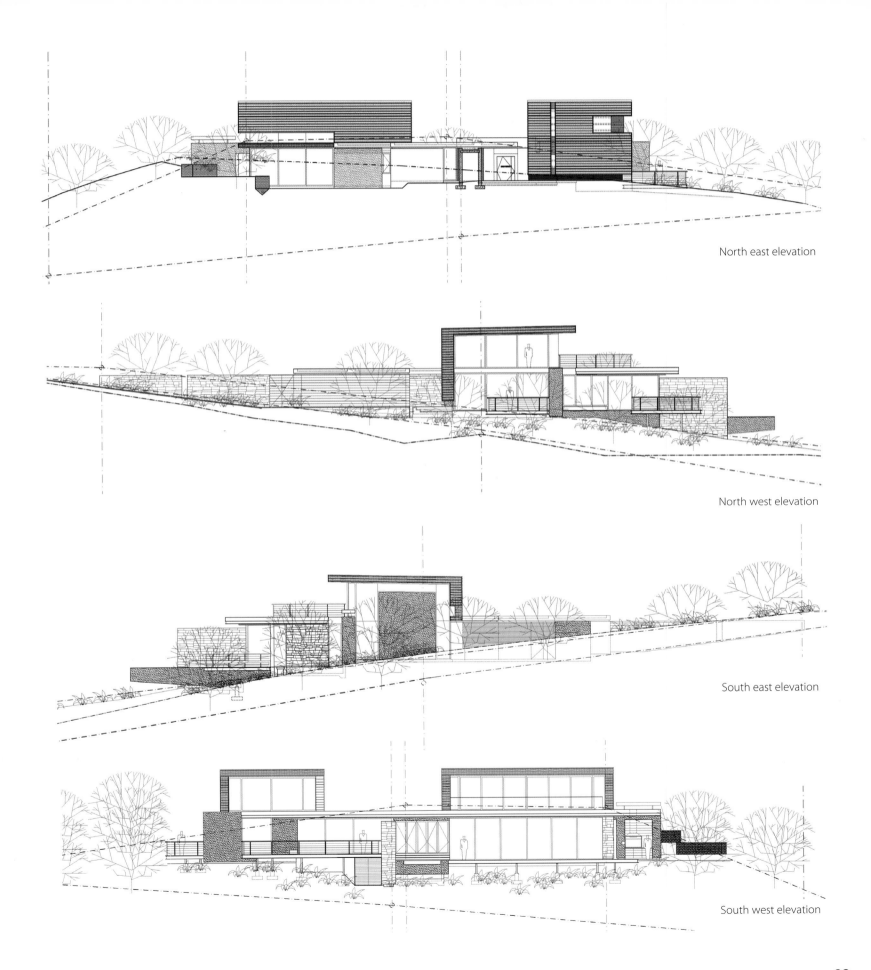

North east elevation

North west elevation

South east elevation

South west elevation

23

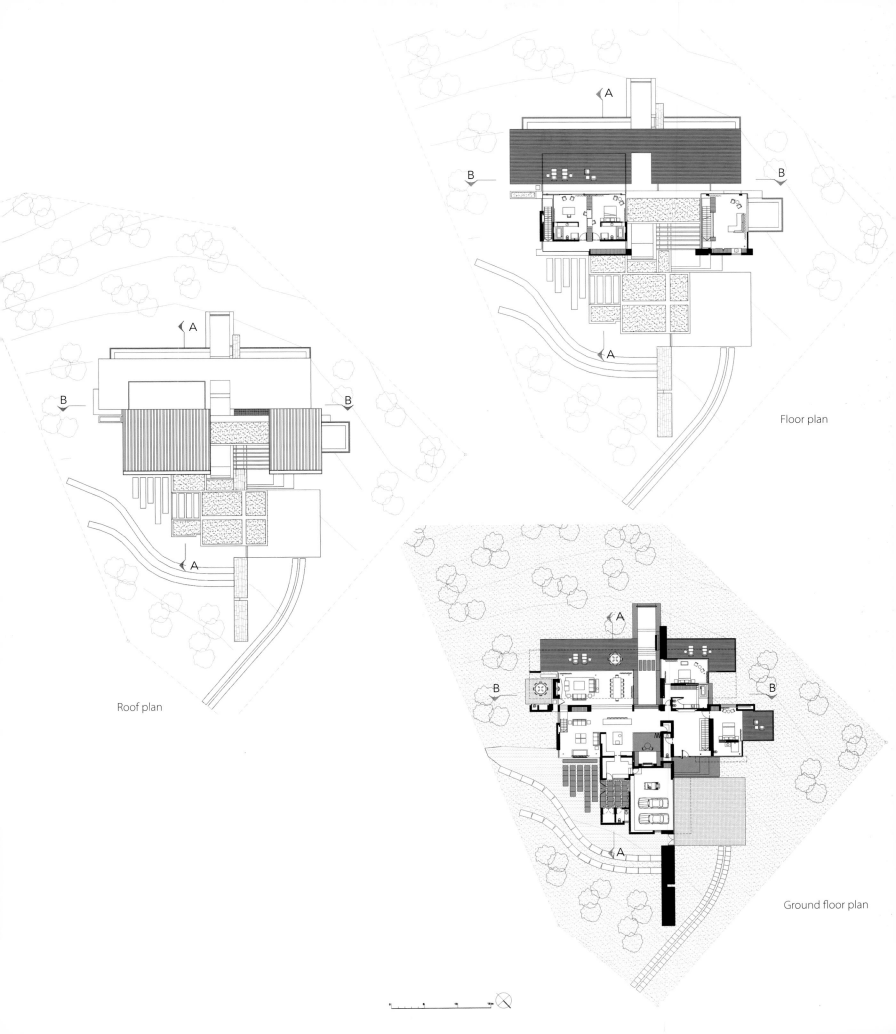

Floor plan

Roof plan

Ground floor plan

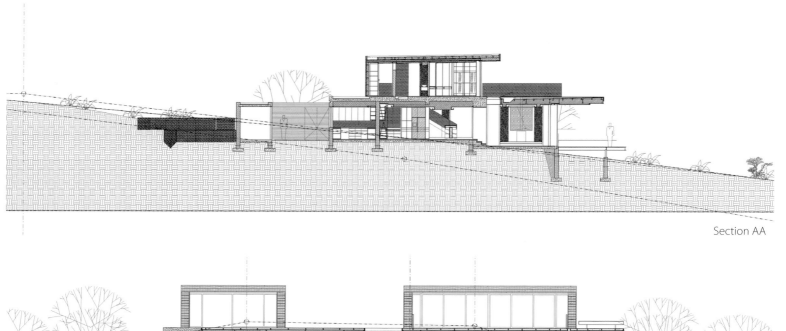

Section AA

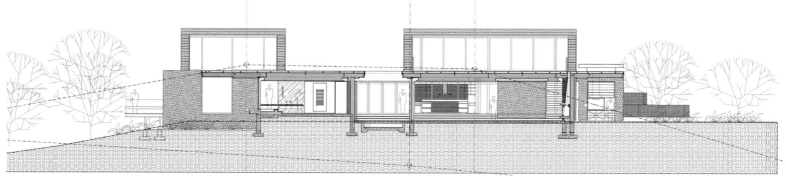

Section BB

A pool connects with the living space, which in turn merges with the interior of the house. From the poolside terrace there are spectacular views of both the sea and the adjacent rolling landscape.

The Apartment

The Apartment YMCA

New York, USA   **Photographs:** Contributed by The Apartment

Architecture:
The Apartment

Superlatively revamped and reconstructed, what was once a YMCA basketball court and suspended running truck has been transformed into a sprawling 650 sqm (7,000 sqft) design loft. Exquisitely outfitted with furniture from the world's most exclusive design studios, what had previously been presented as a raw construction zone is now an architectural and cultural showcase.

The existing trusses throughout the space hint at the former use of this elegant loft, while the re-hauled interior features expanded window openings for a fresher, lighter ambience. The hardwood floor of the old basketball court was also reused, now gracing the private areas of the apartment. Poured concrete is the minimalist flooring chosen for the shared spaces.

Comfort and style were central concerns, as evidenced by the computer controlled lighting, heating and air conditioning systems and sound-insulated floor slabs. No detail was left unattended to in the kitchen, with its Corian countertops and integrated garbage disposal, wine refrigerator, two full-sized refrigerators and two dishwashers.

The apartment enjoys a total of five bedrooms and, in another measure ensuring the maximum degree of comfort, five corresponding full bathrooms. Furthermore, there are two home theaters, a home office and an indoor garden equipped with grow lights.

The master bedroom has three built-in closets and a king-sized walnut bed on a built-in platform. The six-sided, fully tiled master bathroom features two Boffi showers designed by Marcel Wanders, a steam room for two, a freestanding bathtub by Phillipe Starck, and a wall-sized medicine cabinet. A revolving disco ball adds a touch of whimsy in the sprawling walk-in master closet, where the shoe racks can accommodate 100 pairs and where there is a also a built-in vanity and a daybed.

A plush five-person sofa sits opposite a gas fireplace in the great room, which is equipped with floor outlets, an iPod docking station, DJ input station, home theater, concealed kitchenette and a moss rug by Kasthall.

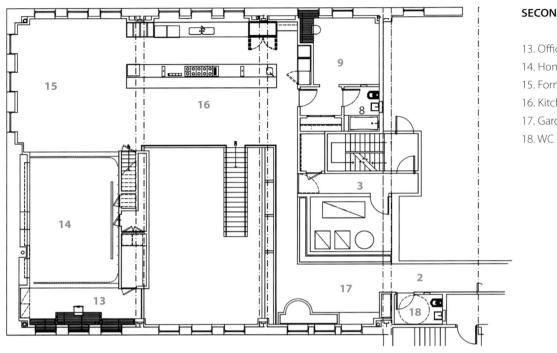

SECOND FLOOR PLAN

13. Office
14. Home theater
15. Formal dining
16. Kitchen
17. Garden
18. WC

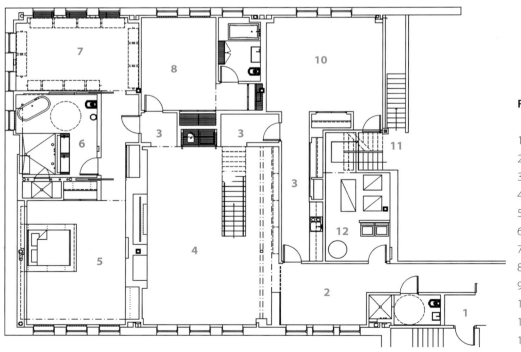

FIRST FLOOR PLAN

1. Lobby
2. Entry
3. Hall
4. Living room
5. Master bedroom
6. Master bathroom
7. Master closet
8. Bedroom
9. Bathroom
10. Design room
11. Fire stair
12. Mechanical room

THIRD FLOOR PLAN

19. Mezzanine bedroom
20. Mezzanine bathroom
21. Open to below

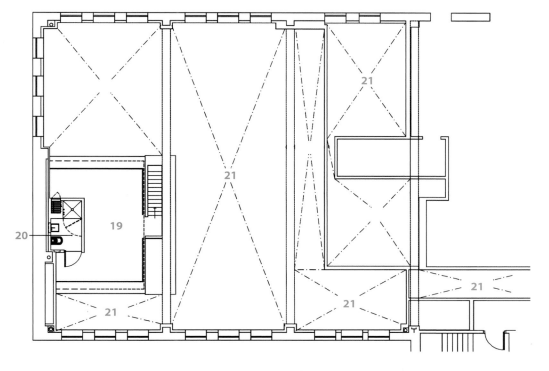

Ettore Sottsass & Johanna Grawunder

Olabuenaga House

Maui, Hawaii, USA

Photographs: Santi Caleca

This project, located on a large and flat piece of land surrounded by tall trees, is divided into a family home of 800 sqm (8,600 sqft), with 3 bedrooms, a kitchen, dining area, living room, study and large central courtyard; and a physical training area of 500 sqm (5,400 sqft) consisting of an indoor pool, sauna/steam bath and exercise rooms.

The organizing elements of the design are the passages that weave through the different spaces, gardens which are voids as well as volumes, exterior materials which follow the movement of the building rather than its volumetric definition, and the natural and artificial lighting that defines the interior spaces using light, color and texture. Together the volumes and voids form an architectural composition that is more like a village in its spatial variety and the complex interactions between the parts than a unitary building.

Architecture:
Ettore Sottsass & Johanna Grawunder
Collaborator:
Richard Young

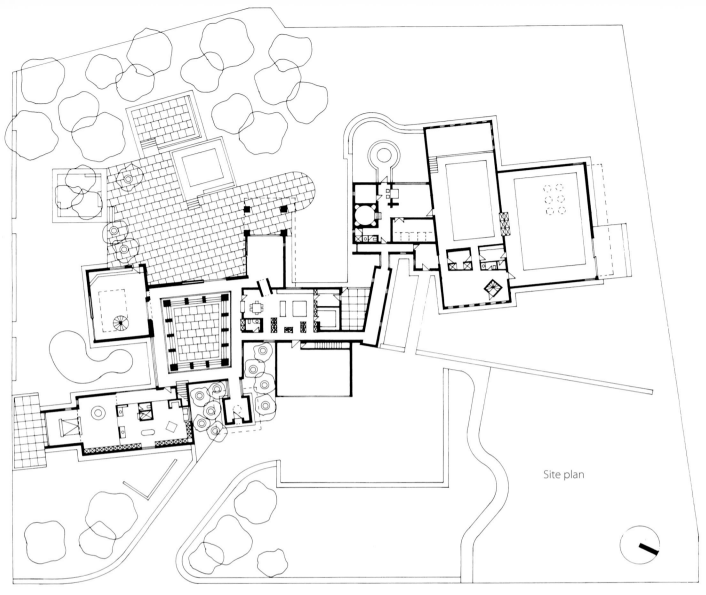

Site plan

The combination of different colors and textures plays a major role in the definition of the spaces. The aim was to obtain a large variety of atmospheres, each with a distinct personality.

Upper floor plan

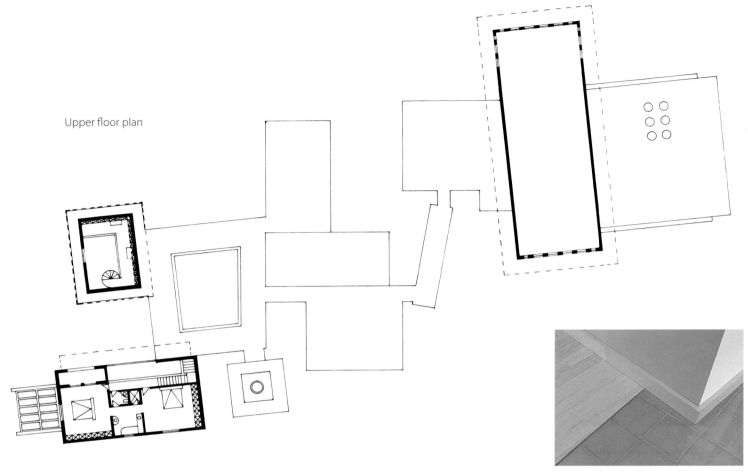

In this dwelling the circulation spaces were treated as environments that not only act as areas of transition between the rooms but also as rooms that articulate the rhythms of the house.

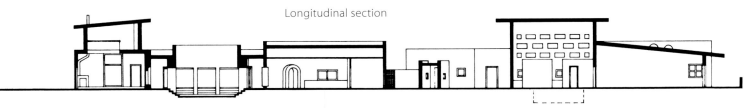

Together the volumes and voids form an architectural complex that is more like a village in its spatial variety than a unitary building.

PROCTER: RIHL

Slice House

Porto Alegre, Brazil   **Photographs:** Marcelo Nunes, Sue Barr

Architecture:
PROCTER: RIHL

The Slice House project was selected to represent Brazil in the IV Latin American Architecture Biennale in October 2004 in Peru. The deisgn contains a series of references to modern Brazilian architecture as well as adding a new element with its complex prismatic geometry which generates a series of spatial illusions in the interior. The house is located on a site measuring 12 feet in width and 126 feet in length (3.7 m X 38.5 m). Having been vacant for more than 20 years, it had already gone to auction 3 times without any interest whatsoever. The present client was the only one to put in an offer on the 4th auction, as the other bidders could not see its potential.

The design of the house uses prismatic geometry with flush details, which demand careful detailing and site supervision. 3D modeling ensured the accuracy and precision of delivered components with final sizing on site. Windows, metalwork, and cabinetwork were assembled on-site. These elements were crafted with delicate precision, in contrast to the intentionally rough concrete surfaces.

In-situ concrete cast agasint timber formwork was chosen for the structural elements of the house as this construction technique is an established tradition in the local area and pre-cast concrete elements or metal formwork are not available for this size of project. The timber formwork was built of rough sawn planks so that the wood grain would be imprinted on the surface of the concrete. The ceilings were cast at an angle of 10 degrees, a common technique in Brazil. The terrace and swimming pool are finished with resin and fiberglass coatings applied on site after the concrete had cured.

Probably the most striking feature of the house is the handcrafted metalwork. The 23 foot long (7 m) kitchen counter is a continuous steel slab with 7 foot (2 m) cantilevered tables at each end towards the dining area and courtyard, respectively. The thick steel plate folds up from the lower dining height to the higher work counter. The steel work surface is coated with avocado-colored, two-part catalyzed laboratory paint providing an extremely hard finish. The stair is realized in folded 5/16 inch (8 mm) steel plate welded in sections onto the undercarriage beams. Since the stair is structurally self-supporting, the design of the balustrade could be especially lightweight.

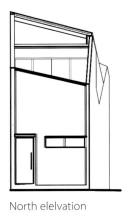

North elelvation

South elelvation

The ceilings were cast at an angle of 10 degrees, a common technique in Brazil. The terrace and swimming pool are finished with resin and fiberglass coatings applied on site after the concrete had cured.

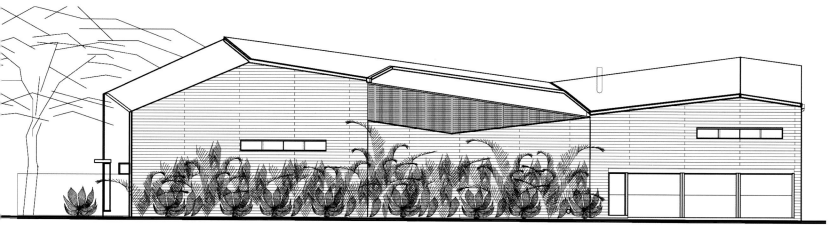

West elelvation

First floor plan

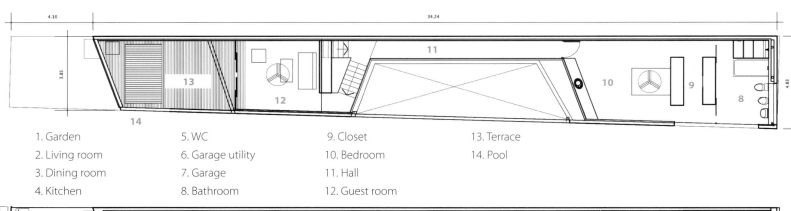

1. Garden	5. WC	9. Closet	13. Terrace
2. Living room	6. Garage utility	10. Bedroom	14. Pool
3. Dining room	7. Garage	11. Hall	
4. Kitchen	8. Bathroom	12. Guest room	

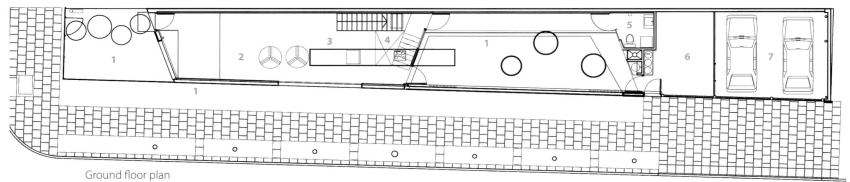

Ground floor plan

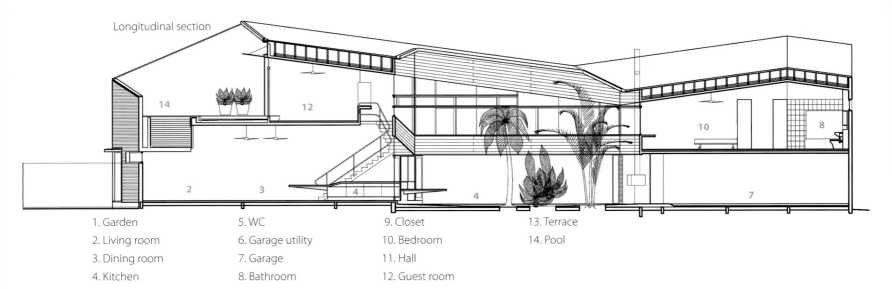

Longitudinal section

14 | 12 | 10 | 8
2 | 3 | 4 | 4 | 7

1. Garden
2. Living room
3. Dining room
4. Kitchen

5. WC
6. Garage utility
7. Garage
8. Bathroom

9. Closet
10. Bedroom
11. Hall
12. Guest room

13. Terrace
14. Pool

© Sue Barr

55

Marco Savorelli

Nicola's Home

Milan, Italy

Photographs: Matteo Piazza

The client and designers were clear from the start about the process to be folllowed in this renovation project for a loft in Milan: to start from zero, working on the abstract functions and utilities of a "home system", beginning from the recovery of a unitarian, primary, elemental space, translating old functions into new, simplified forms.

Functional spaces like the bathroom, kitchen and wardrobe translate themselves into monolithic volumes that, reduced into simple forms, gain sculptural presence.

This is a project where the historical memory of the site meets a rigorous formal approach. The well balanced experimentation with new spaces has been driven by an interest in maintaining the existing qualities of the natural light. The result is a playful alternation of volumes and moods, a fluid exchange between the pre-existing and the new spaces. These are the characteristics of a project which evolved from an intense dialog between the architect and the client, and from an ambition to achieve a minimalist aesthetic coupled with volumetric and functional complexity. This is not simply an interior design project but the creation of volumes to be lived in and for "living with" in an entirely modern and innovative way. The space acquires both a playful and a reflective quality.

When entering the apartment, the visual impact of the delicatley balanced spaces, materiality and lighting is striking. The daylight traces delicate designs on the neat surfaces, while shadows in perpetual movement create a simple and primordial game of light and darkness.

Architecture:
Marco Savorelli
Collaborator:
Luca Mercatelli
Master builders:
Arbusta Arredamenti s.n.c.
(wood construction)
GI.OR.SI Construzioni s.n.l.
Building services engineers:
Zeus Impianti s.n.l.

Light was treated as construction element whose function consisted not only in lighting the dwelling but also in defining spaces inside it. The dominant top lighting gives the spaces a strong verticality.

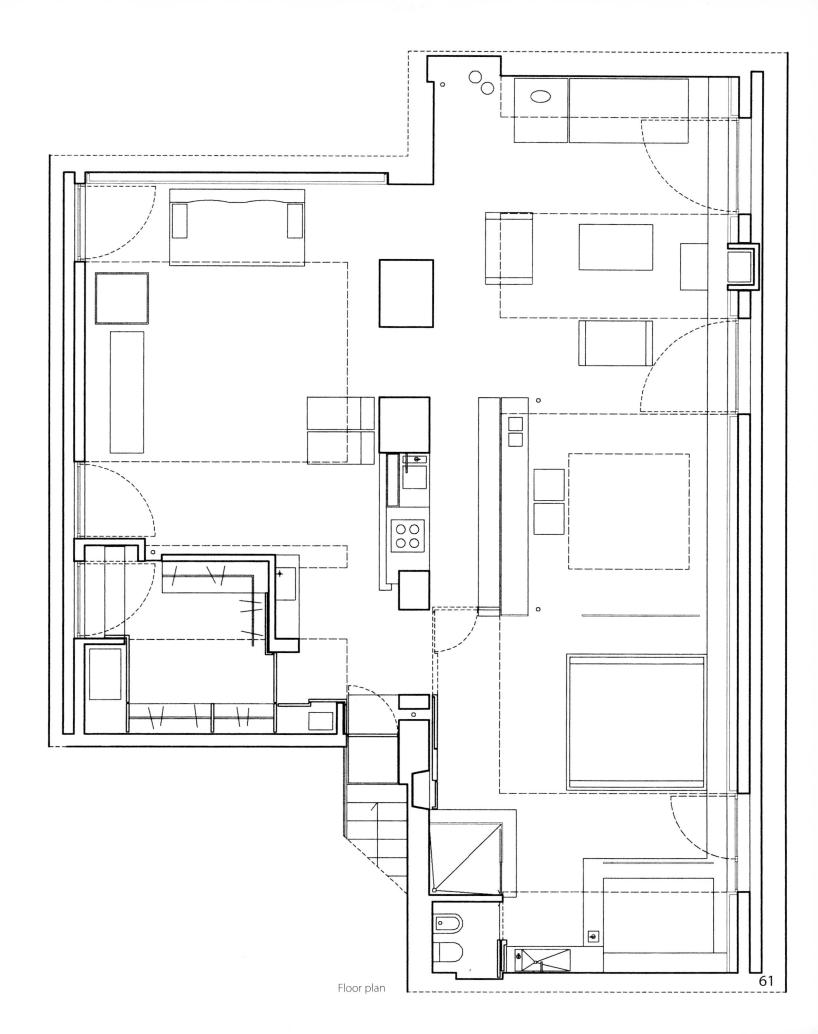

Floor plan

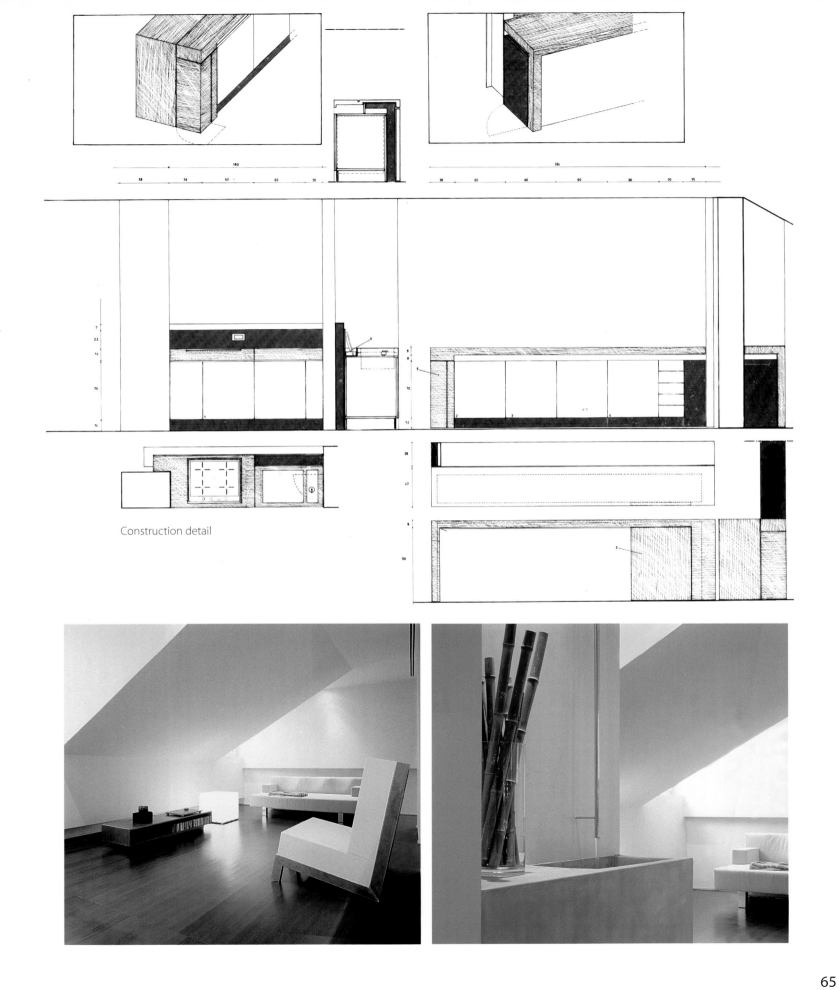

Construction detail

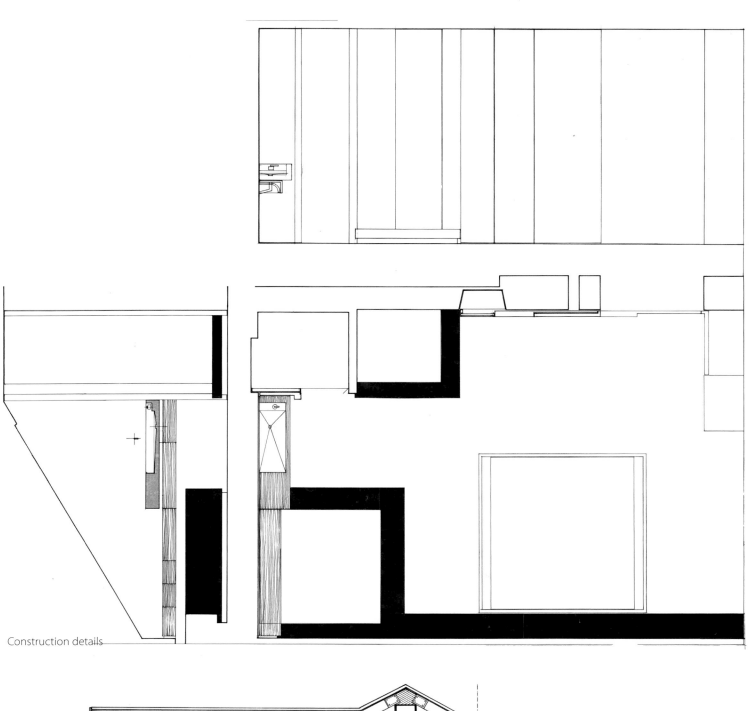

Construction details

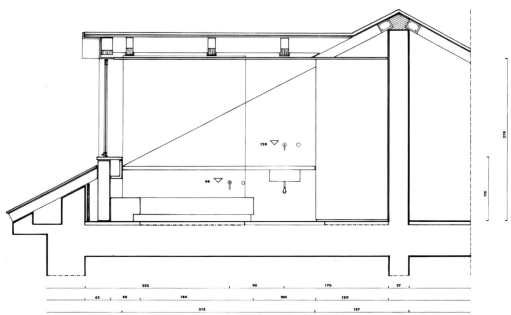

The distribution of spaces follows an open plan, with minimum partitions and a constant search for fluency and dialogue between the different areas.

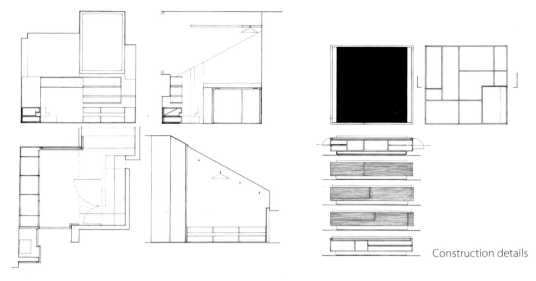

Construction details

Eline Strijkers

Unit 9

Amsterdam, the Netherlands

Photographs: Teo Krijgsman

Architecture:
Eline Strijkers

It is the floor plan that is invariably the dominant plane in the design of the functional distribution of a space, so when Eline Strijkers decided to organize this apartment vertically using a multistory elevation as the point of departure, it was bound to lead to an innovative outcome. In this particular live-work apartment the functions are distributed over the walls rather than floors.

This was the starting point for the refurbishment project for a harbor building (measuring some 2691 sqft or 250 sqm) in Amsterdam-North. All supporting functions are housed in enclosed volumes. Because work, storage, seating, eating, cooking, and sleeping are all components of a particular volume or surface, the space is almost entirely free of freestanding pieces of furniture.

The volumes unfold like independent sculptures, while at the same time making possible a free division of the space. Here, also, a vertical organization of the space is emphasized. There is a clear division between the ground floor and the other levels, which have been handled as a spatial whole.

The radical nature of the spatial concept lies mainly in the way that Strijkers has developed the unexpected materialization of her design, down to the smallest detail. On the ground floor, a change in material was used to mark the transition from one room to another.

The materials used upstairs give terms like 'domesticity' and ' coziness' an entirely new frame of reference. Despite all the attention paid to space, form, materials and details, the rooms are not overwhelmed by a profusion of design. The prevailing casual atmosphere is the result of an unpolished use of materials, a sense of openness between the various parts of this home/workspace and, in particular, the tendency toward collective use.

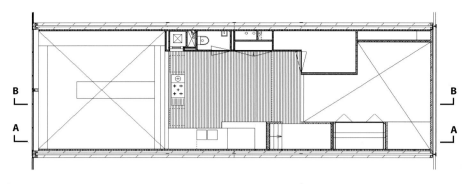

Second floor plan

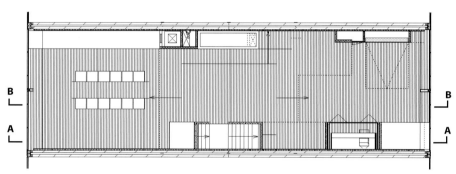

First floor plan

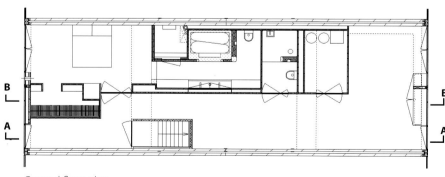

Ground floor plan

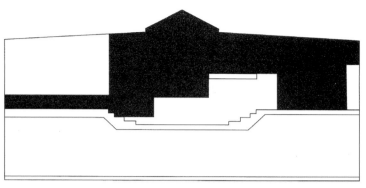

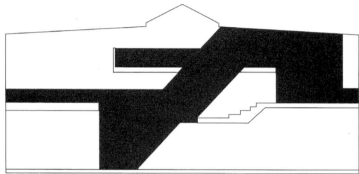

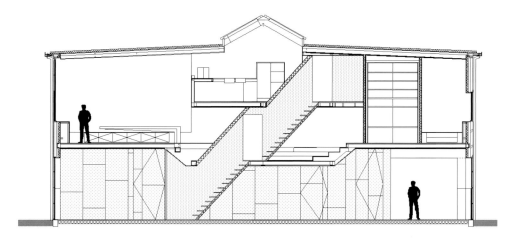

The radical nature of this apartment's spatial concept lies in the way that the functions are distributed over the walls rather than the floors.

Section AA

The work, storage, seating, eating, cooking and sleeping functions are all contained within a particular volume or surface, so the space is almost entirely devoid of freestanding furniture.

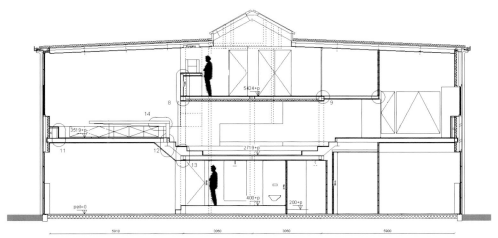

Section BB

Uras + Dilekci Architects

Misir loft

Istanbul, Turkey

Photographs: Ali Bekman

The Misir building, designed by Armenian architect Hovsep Aznavour in 1910, is located in the central Beyoglu district of Istanbul. The brief for this project was to create a 280 sqm (3,000 sqft) loft on the second floor of this building to serve as a second city home for a couple who enjoy entertaining.

With this in mind, the architects focused on retaining some of the original character of the space, while transforming it into a highly original, modern and flexible apartment.

Near the entrance and in the kitchen, the floor was lifted to create a counter which can be used for dining and working. Changing color strips of light were embedded in the floor below, and can be programmed to create different moods. The lighting in most of the house, including a custom made chandelier, is made from simple black electrical wire and hanging lightbulbs, and strategically placed mirrored surfaces create different effects.

The original brick and structural timber was exposed in places in order to keep the original flavor of the building, and the plaster ceilings were burnt with a torch to create an organic texture.

In the bedroom, which can be completely closed off from the rest of the apartment by a 360 degree black velvet curtain, one of the walls is made of glass and the other is a remote controlled, red PVC lacquared door.

In the bathroom, oval marble and steel pieces were cut out and placed into the screed to create a terrazzo-like textured floor, and the cabinets were custom made using bamboo verneer.

Architecture:
Uras + Dilekci Architects

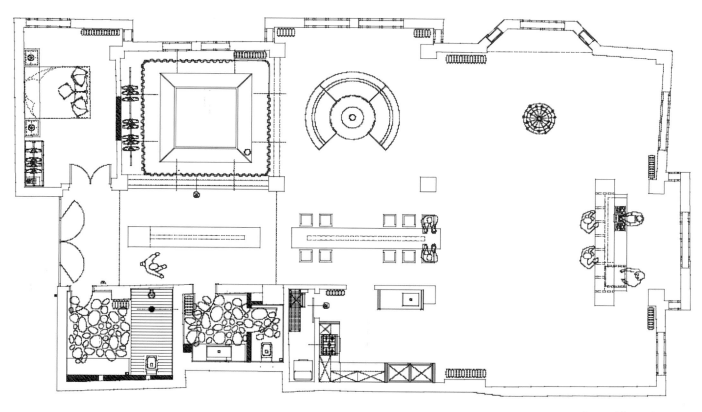

Ground floor plan

The bedroom is the only "closed" space in the apartment, and can be isolated from the rest of the space using black velvet curtains. A green circular dining booth was designed by Atelier Derin to serve more formal dinners in the space, and a screen which slides down over the glass wall separating the bedroom and the dining area can be used for screening films.

Slade Architecture

Apartment in Miami Beach

Miami, Florida, USA

Photographs: Ken Hayden / Redcover.com

This apartment in South Beach, Miami was designed for a young couple as a very "Miami" vacation home. Occupied periodically by the client and occasional guests, the renovation aimed to maximize the ocean views and generate an open, informal atmosphere.

In the original layout two bedrooms were separated from the living room by sheetrock walls coming off the continuous curtain wall so the expansive view was cut into three. A primary objective of the intervention was to free the whole width of the curtain wall, and use materials and colors to suggest the continuation of the interior into the exterior.

To achieve this openness and yet retain the bedrooms, two transformable walls were designed, a moving wall unit and a pivoting wall. They provide a dynamic, flexible way of configuring the space so the bedrooms can be incorporated into the main living space, creating a much bigger area, and the windows and views are shared between the spaces.

The guest room has a storage closet partition wall which hangs from the ceiling and slides out from the demising wall to create a bedroom. When folded and closed the space becomes part of the living area. Operated by a removable crank-driven mechanism, the wall incorporates drawers, a hanging space and the door to the bedroom and can conceal the Murphy Bed mounted on the demising wall. A 10 foot wide full-height pivoting wall was created for the master bedroom which opens so the window can be seen from the living area while protecting the bedroom's privacy.

Corners were rounded off to create a continuous flowing space that starts in the entry and ends in this operable pivot wall, accentuating the depth of the apartment.

The bed and the cantilevered desk in the master bedroom were designed in 3D, then manufactured from solid blocks of foam reinforced with steel and aluminum and covered in a lacquer finished, fiberglass skin. This finish is reminiscent of a surfboard, in keeping with the environment and the client's personal interest in surfing. The desk is anchored to a floor-to-ceiling steel column embedded in the millwork. The bed shape derived from morphing a flower shaped base into a rectangular bed. The underside and shape of this bed are important because they are reflected in the glossy resin floor. It is a loose piece of furniture that sits on the floor.

The finish materials were carefully chosen to accentuate the view and internalize the ocean, sky and sand: the blue custom resin floor has a sand-like texture with a smooth surface while the translucent curtains enhance the blue and the glossy white walls reflect the ocean. The interior view, with its rosewood paneling and warmer colors, emphasizes solidity in contrast with the bright finishes on the ocean side.

Architecture:
Slade Architecture
General contractor:
Edward Nieto Design Group
Moving wall unit fabricator:
Jesus Tejedor
Stereo A/V:
Red Rose (NY)/ Interseckt (Miami)
Fiberglass desk and bed:
Slade Architecture (Design) and Tom McGuire (Fabrication)
Resin floors:
Fusion Floors
Curtains:
Deco Center
Furnishings:
Slade Architecture

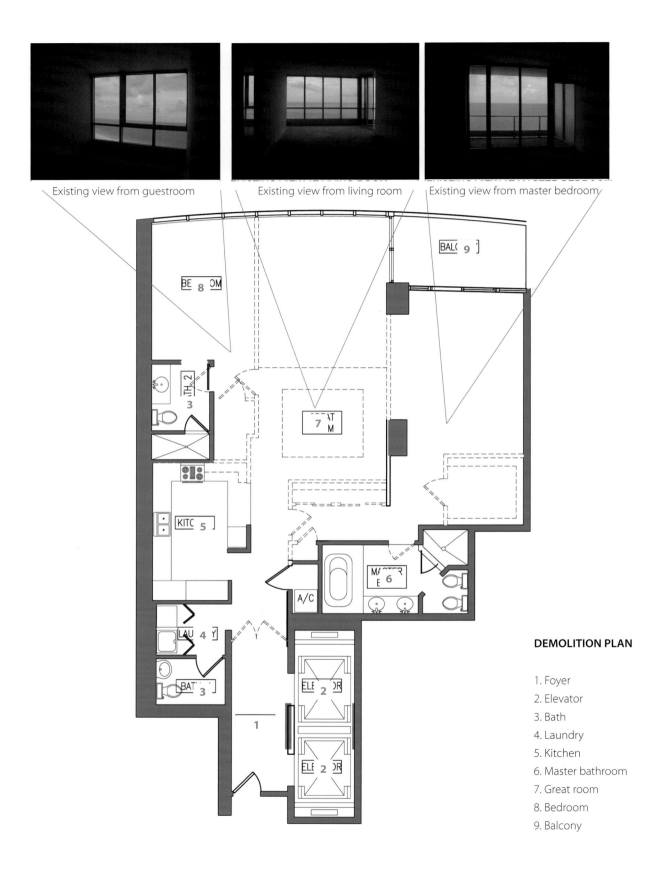

Existing view from guestroom

Existing view from living room

Existing view from master bedroom

BAL 9

BE 8 OM

TH 2 3

7 AT M

KITC 5

MASTER E 6

A/C

LAU 4 Y

BAT 3

ELE 2 OR

ELE 2 OR

1

DEMOLITION PLAN

1. Foyer
2. Elevator
3. Bath
4. Laundry
5. Kitchen
6. Master bathroom
7. Great room
8. Bedroom
9. Balcony

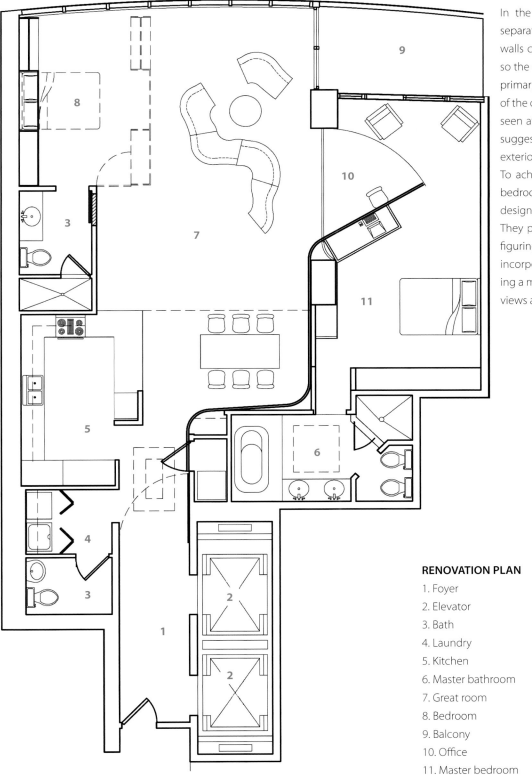

In the original layout two bedrooms were separated from the living room by sheetrock walls coming off the continuous curtain wall so the expansive view was cut into three. The primary objective was to free the whole width of the curtain wall so all the windows could be seen at once, using materials and colors that suggest a continuation of the interior into the exterior.

To achieve this openness and yet retain the bedrooms, two transformable "walls" were designed, a moving wall unit and a pivot wall. They provide a dynamic, flexible way of configuring the space so the bedrooms can be incorporated into the main living space, creating a much bigger area, and the windows and views are shared between spaces.

RENOVATION PLAN

1. Foyer
2. Elevator
3. Bath
4. Laundry
5. Kitchen
6. Master bathroom
7. Great room
8. Bedroom
9. Balcony
10. Office
11. Master bedroom

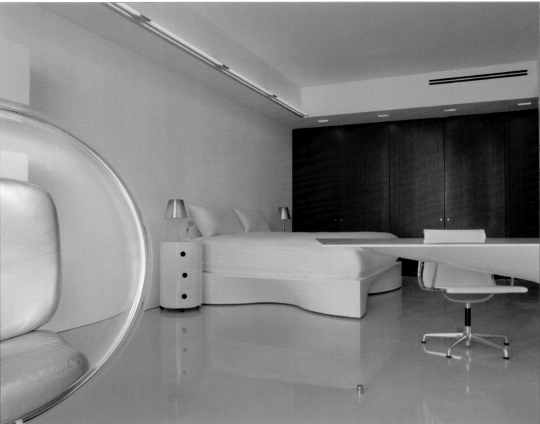

The finishing materials were carefully chosen to accentuate the view and internalize the ocean, sky and sand: the blue custom resin floor has a sand-like texture with a smooth surface while the translucent curtains enhance the blue and the glossy white walls reflect the ocean. The interior view, with its rosewood paneling and warmer colors, emphasizes solidity in contrast with the bright finishes on the ocean side.

UID architects

Rustic House

Fukuyama City, Hiroshima, Japan

Photographs: Hiroshi Ueda

This site near Fakuyama City in the Hiroshima prefecture is set in a peaceful and calm rural environment, where the foot of a nearby mountain opens into wide open plains used for agricultural purposes. The brief given to Japanese architect Keisuke Maeda, founder of UID architects, was for a residence that would be used by a young couple. The home was to be built on the site where the wife's parents were already living.

The plot's level differences, which have been largely formed by the existing stone wall terraces, have been used to great advantage in defining the various domestic functions of the building. They generate natural separations between the different areas and create a labyrinthine interior, which breaks from more standard housing typologies. The trees which already existed on the site were also incorporated into the finished house.

On the west side of the property the architects have fitted a louver set at an irregular angle. This element acts as a buffer between interior and exterior, drawing light in and allowing a gentle connection to be established with the natural surroundings. It also provides views, when desired, of the adjacent residence where the client's parents live.

This transitional space connects the living room with the semi-open plan dining and kitchen area and has an exterior aesthetic thanks to the expansive glazed surfaces, the louver and the gravel finish on the floor.

The architects chose wood as the predominant external finish to integrate with the natural texture of the stone wall. The rustic quality of the wood transmits the age of the walls and reflects the tranquility of the surrounding countryside. Cedar board was employed for the façade thanks to its long-term durability and texture. The wood was treated and dried to achieve a water content of below 15%. This significantly hardens the material and lessens foundation tensions. The surface of the wood boasts a rich texture, which is complemented by the pattern generated by the crosspieces that join the boards.

Architecture:
UID architects
Principal architect:
Keisuke Maeda
General contractor:
Norikazu Okita
Structural design:
Teruaki Tanaka
Landscape architect:
Zenjiro Hashimoto
Mechanical systems:
Kousou Katayama

The house makes use of the existing stone piling, allowing the level differences to define interior functions and layouts.

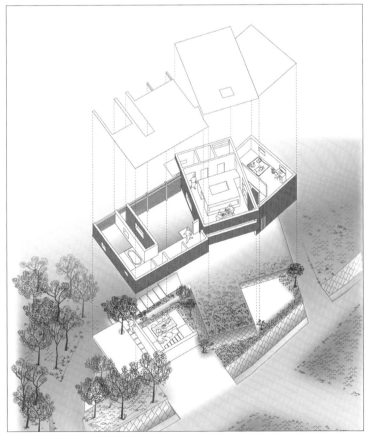

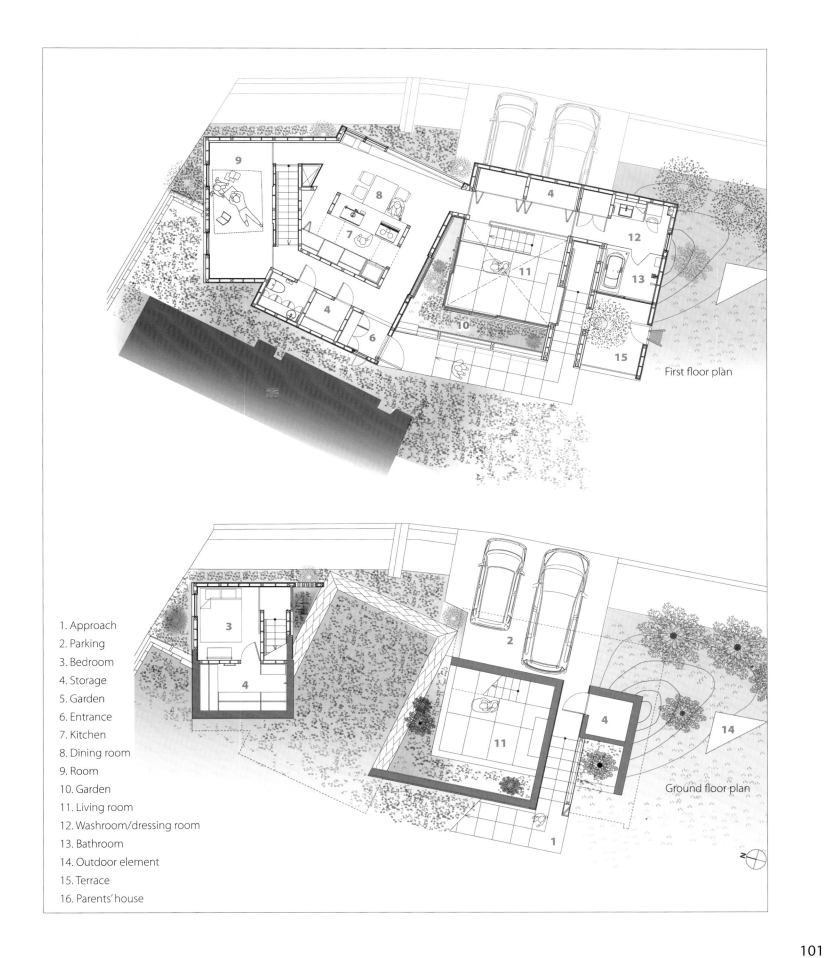

First floor plan

1. Approach
2. Parking
3. Bedroom
4. Storage
5. Garden
6. Entrance
7. Kitchen
8. Dining room
9. Room
10. Garden
11. Living room
12. Washroom/dressing room
13. Bathroom
14. Outdoor element
15. Terrace
16. Parents' house

Ground floor plan

A panoramic window in the dining room affords views over the house's rural setting, which can also be enjoyed from the work area in the adjacent kitchen.

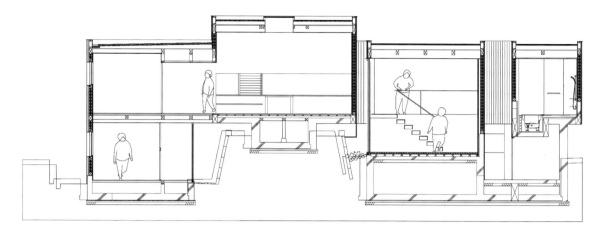

Edwards Moore

The Cubby House

Melbourne, Australia

Photographs: contributed by Edwards Moore

Architecture:
Edwards Moore

Architects Edwards Moore used unusual materials, such as OSB, and innovative angles to create a well-communicated, spacious, light, modern interior. The architects' intention was to enhance and add an extension to an already existing apartment overlooking a public swimming pool. Named Cubby House, the designers rid the space of walls and doors, providing a floor plan with greater flexibility and sustainability. An extra, upper floor was added to house a bedroom and bathroom.

The lower level of the house is designated for the more public functions. Edwards Moore raised the original ceiling to allow room for the injected elevated kitchen floor. The kitchen platform is the first step for the staircase, which wraps up from behind the kitchen island and along the window wall. The stairway is supported by a rhythm of pillars that cast interesting shadows seen when viewed from outside. The lobby entrance encased inside a gold box also serves as storage for wine bottles and acts as a privacy screen for the toilet.

The upper level addition is constructed of steelwork that is left partly exposed on the ceiling of the double-height space. The top floor is filled with light from the skylights above and from the windows overlooking the pool outside. The bedroom wardrobe creates a corridor walkway from the stairs to the bathroom. Glazed panels in the bathroom reflect the natural light coming from the circular skylight for a heightened natural light experience. The bedroom wardrobe is wrapped in three OSB panels and has a gold reflective front that can rotate to create a new small study or guest bedroom space. There is also an outdoor terrace on the upper level that is intimately connected to the bedroom space and is designed to enhance natural ventilation through the house.

Edwards Moore designed Cubby House's interior to have high polished sharp lines contrasting with rough and tactile surfaces. The designers stuck to a fairly neutral palette with occasional splashes of saturated color from natural wood sources. The materials include reclaimed limed timber, OSB, sisal, vic ash and the floors are finished in white concrete.

The project is filled with reclaimed materials, features transforming spaces that serve multiple functions, and has reflective surfaces that increase indoor natural lighting.

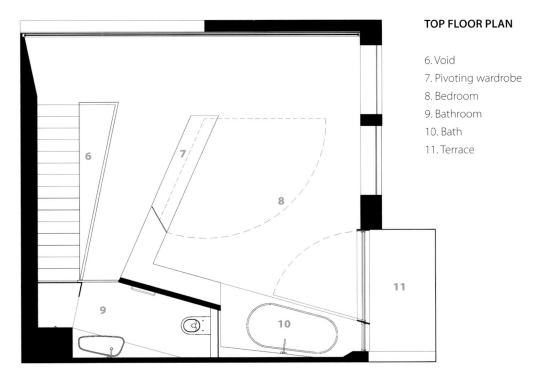

TOP FLOOR PLAN

6. Void
7. Pivoting wardrobe
8. Bedroom
9. Bathroom
10. Bath
11. Terrace

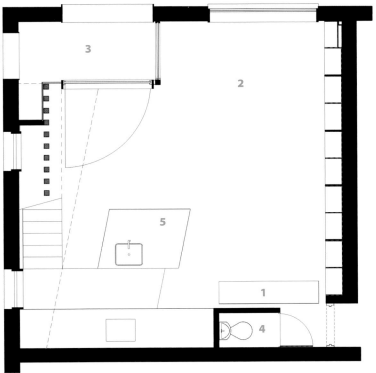

GROUND FLOOR PLAN

1. Sliding reflective box
2. Living space
3. Courtyard
4. Toilet
5. Kitchen

New steelwork provides the structure for the new roof form, with a double height void running through the house to the new roof skylight. Left partly exposed, the steelwork and bracing create a dynamic with the new roof form.

Smith-Miller + Hawkinson

Greenberg Loft

New York, USA

Photographs: Matteo Piazza

The project is a series of interventions, each dedicated to a unique set of local circumstances with particular emphasis on the attention to detail and materiality.

Located in Manhattan´s Garment District at the top of an anonymous concrete building, this project houses the largest private collection of "Outsider Art" as well as a residence for the owner.

Using an austere palate of glass, concrete, blackened steel, and a minimum amount of wood details, significant changes were made to the existing context. At the same time, the existing concrete shell of the loft was treated as a palimpsest for the new work.

Areas for the display of the art collection were developed to coexist with the living program. In light of the owner's varied programs of use, we proposed "cross-programmed" spaces, the definition of which was created by lighting, very large (or moving) doors, and mechanised skylight shades.

Given the sectional constraints of the existing spaces, a new mezzanine floor was added of reinforced concrete. Spectacular views of the city were offered by a rehabilitated north-facing skylight monitor, and new glass and steel handrails were installed along with thin, structural bar hangers to support the mezzanine.

Architecture:
Smith-Miller + Hawkinson
Collaborator:
Henry Smith-Miller, Eric Vand De Sluys,
Maria Ibañez de Sendadiano
Master builders:
Martin Myers Construction

Main plan

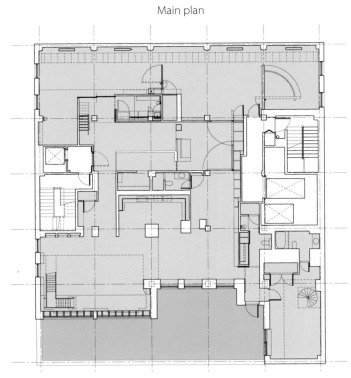

Screening room door partitions-Plan

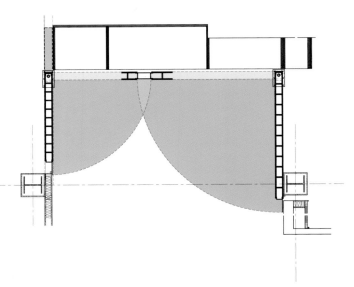

Mezzanine

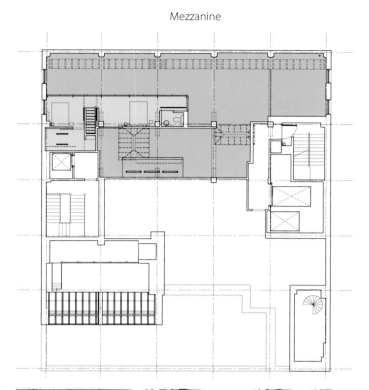

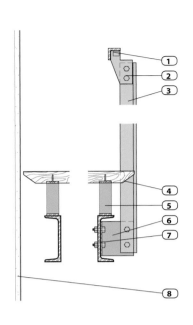

Staircase to mezzanine - elevation

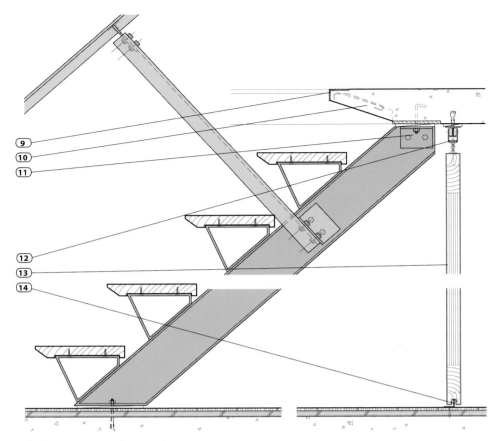

Staircase to mezzanine - section

1. 1 1/2 x1 1/2 x1/4 in. blackened steel angle handrail
2. 1/4 in. steel handrail web
3. 2 x2 x3/8 in. steel post
4. 1 1/2 in. solid maple tread
5. 2 x1/4 in. steel strap

6. 4 x3 x 1/4 in. steel clip bolted to channel
7. C8 x11.5 steel channel
8. Plaster wall
9. 1 1/2 x2 1/2 x1/8 in. steel embedment plate
10. Concrete slab with tapered nosing

11. 4 x 4 x 1/4 x 4 in. steel angle, bolt to steel channel and secure to embedment plate
12. Scheduled door track
13. 1 1/2 in. Maple veneer sliding door leaf
14. 3/4 x 3/4 x 1/8 in. steel door guide, bolt to floor

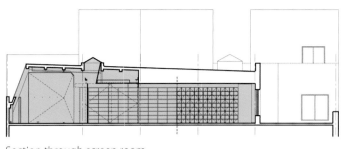

Section through screen room

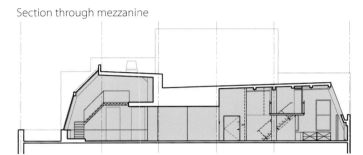

Section through mezzanine

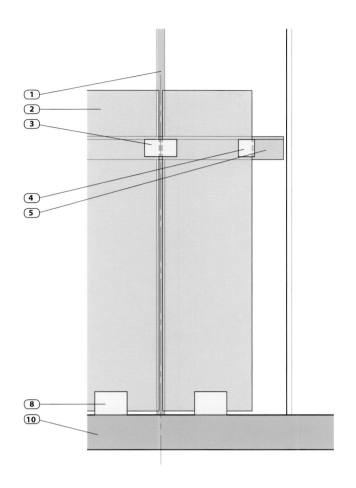

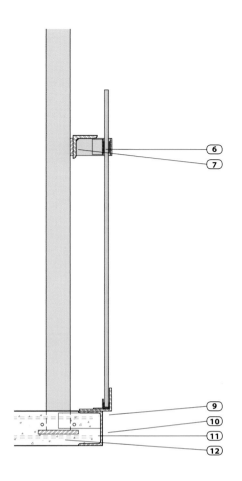

1. 1 x 3 in. blackened steel suspension column
2. 1/2 in. tempered glass
3. WT 5 x 6 x 2 1/4 in. welded to clip
4. 5 x 6 x 2 1/4 in. steel angle welded to clip
5. 3 x 3 x 3/8 in. steel angle handrail
6. 1 3/4 x 1 3/4 x 1/8 in. steel clip
7. 3/8 in. thick steel shim
8. 3 x 4 x 1/4 x 4 in. steel angle
9. 13/4 x 1 3/4 x 1/8 in. steel clip
10. mc4 x 13.8 steel channel cap anchored to slab
11. 2 x 1/4 in. steel strap / tira de acero 2 x 1/4 in.
12. 5 x 1/2 in. steel anchor plate
13. 3/4 in. maple end cap at plaster wall
14. extent of sliding door path

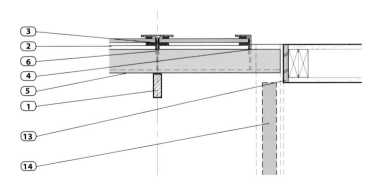

Mezzanine handrail plan

Claesson Koivisto Rune

No.5 House

Nacka, Sweden

Photographs: Åke E:son Lindman

The starting point for this house for a graphic designer and his family (the client designed the No. 5 sign himself) was a simple structure where the inside would be as important as the outside. The design was developed as a geometric volume, a kind of inverted volume that can be read either as a box with a series of openings, or an open space with a series of closures.

The construction method involved establishing a grid based on standard dimensions for building materials, and then superimposing it onto the basic box structure. This grid was used to create the basic room structure for the house, which included three bedrooms, a bathroom and one larger living/dining space with kitchen. One of the four sides of each of the main rooms was completely glazed, allowing natural light into the house and blurring the distinction between interior and exterior. The bedrooms and living area are basically open towards one cardinal point each, meaning there is an opening in each facade. Even though the bedrooms are quite small, the surrounding landscape becomes part of the space, creating a sense of vastness. The bathroom, which has no wall opening, has a roof window instead. A glazed doorway leading out from the living area to a partially walled terrace creates an outdoor room that is open to the sky at one end and open to the view at the other.

Architecture:
Claesson Koivisto Rune

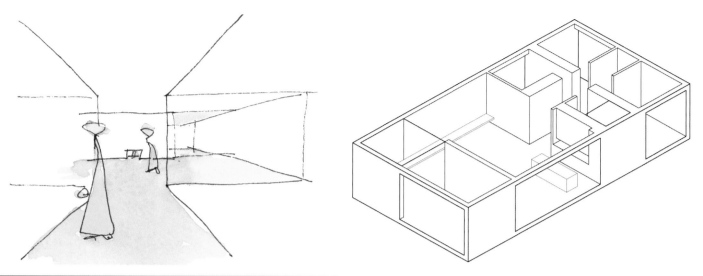

FLOOR PLAN

1. Entrance
2. Bedroom
3. Master bedroom
4. Kitchen
5. Living
6. Terrace

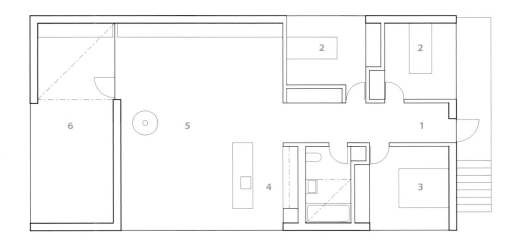

Christian Pottgiesser

24, Rue Buisson Saint Louis

Paris, France   **Photographs:** Luc Boegly

Architecture:
Christian Pottgiesser

This small plot of some thirty-plus square meters (323+ sqft) is surrounded on three and a half sides by the blind walls of neighboring buildings, a condition which limited the possibilities for achieving natural lighting. On the remaining side, an imposing five-story building made for very undesirable views. The architect has created a efficient central space free of clutter and defined by three key elements. First, a large area of glazing with doors opens the apartment to a small courtyard and allows abundant natural light into the interior. A 'strip' housing the living functions is built along the blind side walls. Built into this unit are alcoves set aside for eating, resting, reading, and so forth, as well as the bathroom. The end of the plot is occupied by the bedroom. Finally, a folded, reinforced concrete surface hangs within the space, separated from the side walls of the apartment to let strips of natural light spill down into the interior. It forms an accesible roof, while also blocking out undesirable views.

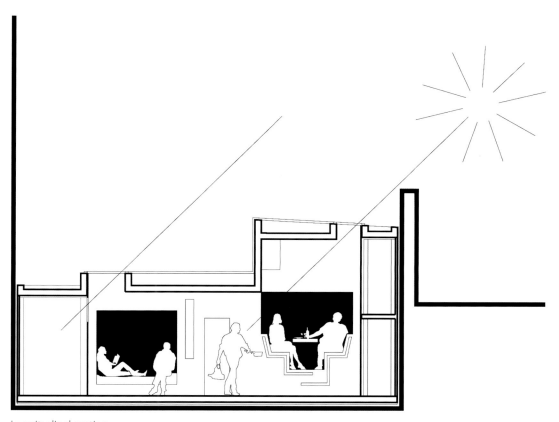

Longitudinal section

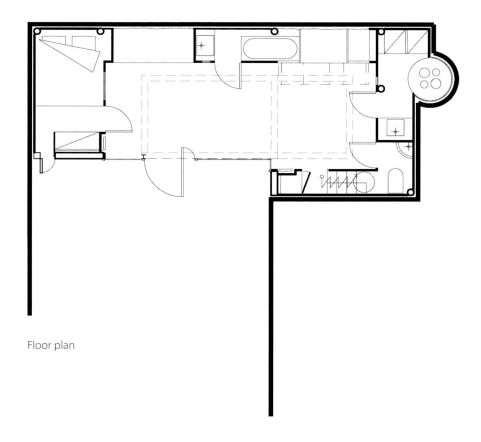

Floor plan

Platform 5

Mapledene Road

Hackney, London, UK   **Photographs:** Alan Williams

Mapledene Road is situated in a conservation area in the up-and-coming district of Hackney, East London. The property forms part of a terrace of houses whose yellow London brick architecture is typical of this part of the capital. The refurbishment was conceived of as a landscape of interventions and new components, which revitalize the property and restore a cozy homeliness to its interior. The cellular ground floor was opened up and extended to the rear to allow the spaces to flow into each other and to the garden, strengthening the connection between the interior and exterior, and allowing the back garden to be used as an additional living space. The existing layout of the first floor, however, was largely retained.

Each room has been designed to maintain a highly individual character, which affords a varied experience as one moves through the house. The kitchen and patio areas are unified by a power-floated concrete floor and London stock brick garden wall giving the internal space an external character. The existing flank wall has been removed and the kitchen is applied as a lining to the rough brickwork. A modern structural glass oriel window lined with cherry wood projects into the garden and juxtaposes with the Victorian bay that projects into the street.

The expansive glass roof over the kitchen opens up the view to the sky, allowing those inside to see planes flying overhead, as well as birds as they swoop down hunting for flies. Daylight is brought in from above to illuminate previously dark spaces and the walls, floors, roof, glazing and appliances have been upgraded to modern standards to maximize insulation and efficiency. Overheating and glare in the kitchen is managed by shading from the surrounding buildings and trees, high thermal mass and the use of solar-control glass and blinds.

Mapledene Road was shortlisted for an RIBA Award, Grand Designs Award and Architects' Journal Small Projects Award. It was also the overall winner in New London Architecture's "Don't Move Improve" competition for the best extension in London.

Architecture:
Platform 5
Structural engineer:
MBOK

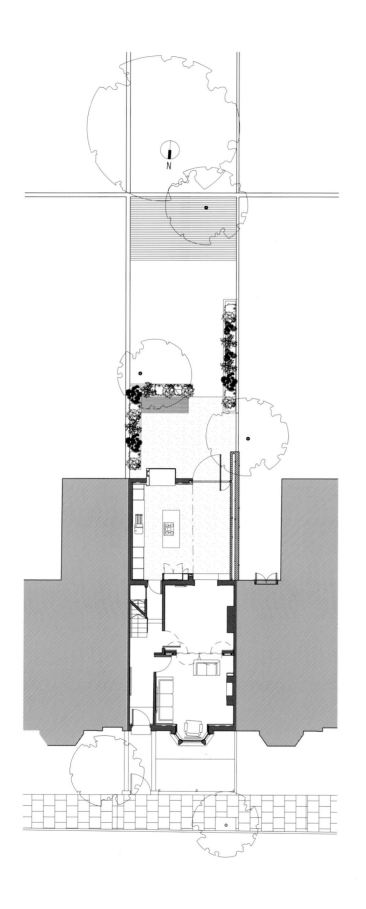

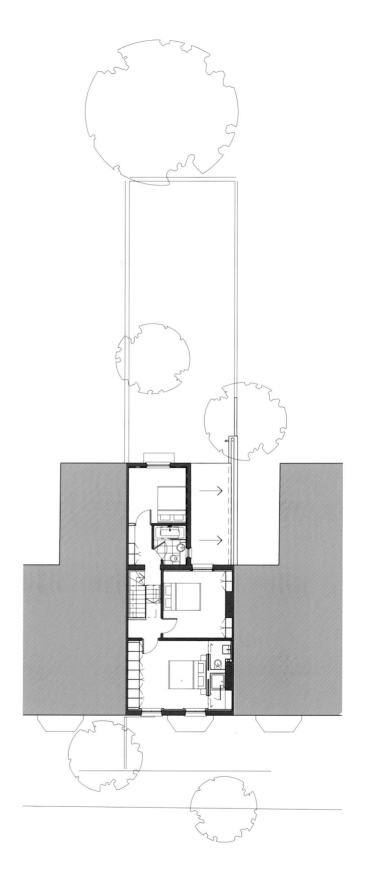

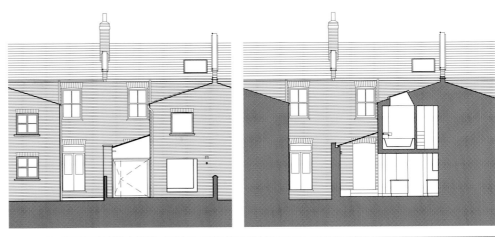

The dining room wall makes use of what was originally the bare brick wall of the back yard. Together with the extensive glazing used for this part of the house, this blurs the distinction between outside and inside.

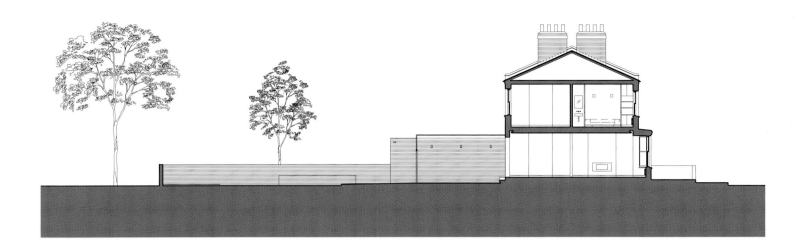

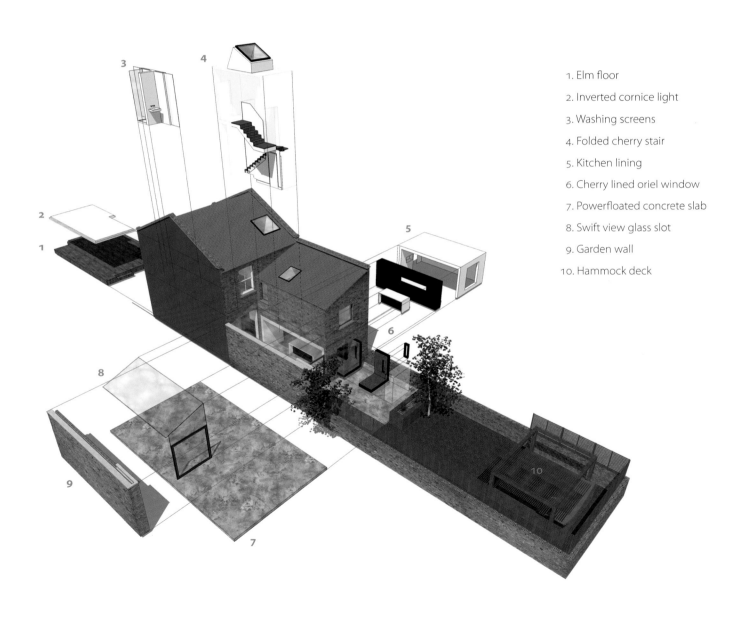

1. Elm floor

2. Inverted cornice light

3. Washing screens

4. Folded cherry stair

5. Kitchen lining

6. Cherry lined oriel window

7. Powerfloated concrete slab

8. Swift view glass slot

9. Garden wall

10. Hammock deck

All appliances and finishes have been chosen to maximize efficiency and thus reduce the running costs of the property.

Adrià+Broid+Rojkind

Casa F2

Mexico City, Mexico

Photographs: Undine Pröhl

Architecture:
Adrià+Broid+Rojkind

This single-family home is located in the outskirts of the metropolitan area of Mexico City. An "L" -shaped floor plan has been adapted to a triangular plot while capturing the best views and avoiding those of the neighboring houses. A circulation axis provides the schematic structure of the house, from the entrance to the linear stairway that joins the three floors, which are located in a single wing of the home. A concrete "box" with perforations is inserted between the two lightweight slabs of the perpendicular body, its opacity and solidity contrasting with the transparency and lightness of the planes that make up the house. The house is set along the slope of the terrain, such that the overhang of some of the concrete planes provides shade in the summer while allowing sunlight to penetrate the interior in the winter. The clients, a young couple planning a family, wanted a house that would be open enough to be able to enjoy its integration in the surrounding natural landscape, but without sacrificing intimacy. A TV and movie room were added to the entrance/service areas and living/dining room, which are all located on the access level. The bedrooms are on the upper floor, while the study and library are on the lower.

From the very first stages of sketching and modeling, the clarity and straightforwardness of the design was given great importance by the architects. This avoidance of ornamentation, with the superposition of finishing materials over the rough foundation, has meant that structural elements have come to form part of the building envelope and the same finishes are used for both interior and exterior surfaces. The concrete slabs comprising the access level and roof have an inverted slope that enhances their lightweight aspect, thereby emphasizing the streamlined horizontal lines. The area abutting the study and library on the lower floor frees up a flat space with a grassy garden area that is suitable for all kinds of domestic activities and festive occasions. Furthermore, the garden has designed to visually blend in with the nearby federally protected reserve land. An outdoor jacuzzi is located at one end and, at the back of the house, a patio serves as an exterior dining area and water mirror. A number of existing trees were left in place in the entrance area: growing out of perforations in the concrete slab they create a welcoming shade at the home's entryway.

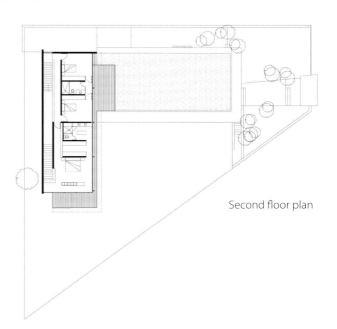

Second floor plan

First floor plan

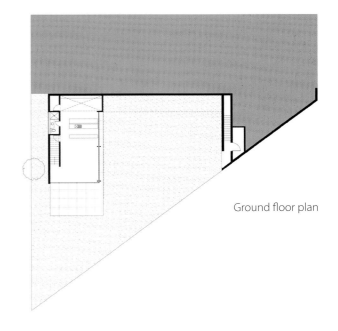

Ground floor plan

151

Clear, simple strategies have been used in the structural design and in the specification of materials and finishes. Special attention was paid to the timber formwork, which was constructed of narrow pine planks to give a rich texture on the interior and exterior surfaces of the cast concrete.

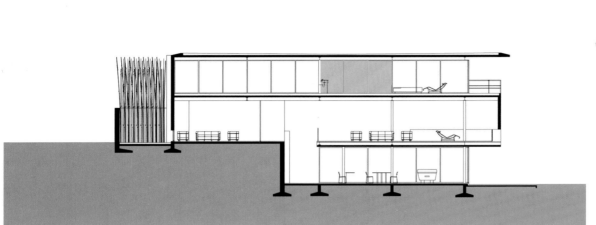

Marc
(Michele Bonino & Subhash Mukerjee) & Federica Patti, Martina Tabò

House in Turin

Turin, Italy

Photographs: Beppe Giardino

A couple in their thirties bought an elegant corner apartment in a 19th century building in the center of Turin. The apartment was very spacious and had interesting views towards a large landscaped boulevard.

The main problem of the remodeling that Coex were asked to design was the big, dark entrance: the clients loved its finely worked continuous terrazzo floor and of course wanted to make it a pleasing and functional space. On the other hand it had no windows and received no natural light. Coex decided to make that space the core and engine of the whole flat.

The entrance is invaded by a massive volume containing "dark functions" - a shower and some storage space. To preserve the integrity of the floor, the volume "flies" one meter above it and the contained functions are only accessible from the back. The volume also serves as a huge lamp for the entrance providing direct illumination throughout this level. To take advantage of the views and to enhance the apartment's sense of spaciousness, the two requested bathrooms are compressed behind the volume. In accordance with the clients' brief, the other rooms have been left almost undesigned, thus emphasizing the contrast between the dark and dense private areas and the light-filled, airy living spaces.

Architecture:
Marc
(Michele Bonino & Subhash Mukerjee) with
Federica Patti, Martina Tabò

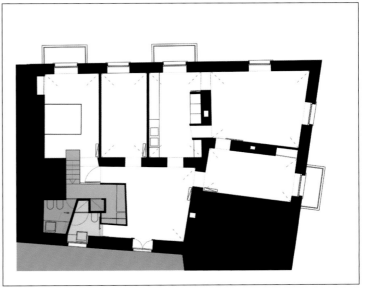

159

The kitchen is well-communicated with the living/dining area, although visually separated by a fixed unit housing kitchen equipment and appliances. All of the flooring in this area is the apartment's original oak parquet.

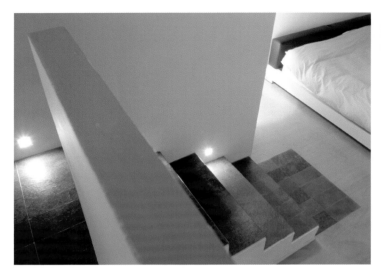

The stairs to the bathroom are paved in dark Brazilian ferrous slate, with the warm beech plywood flooring of the master bedroom set in gentle counterpoint.

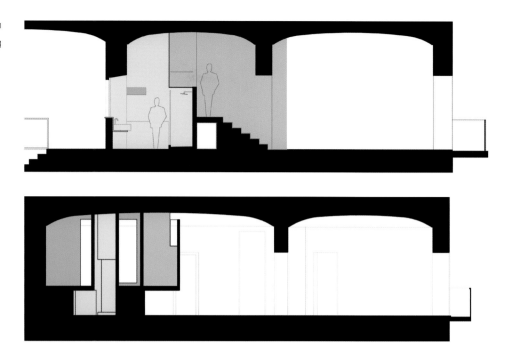

Cho Slade Architecture

Hochhauser Residence

New York, USA

Photographs: Jordi Miralles

Architecture:
Cho Slade Architecture

The brief for the renovation of what is now a 2,400-square-foot apartment (there were originally two apartments dating from the 1960s, each measuring 1,200 sqft or 111 sqm) was as precise as it was varied. The original apartments had to be unified into a single volume for a couple with two daughters, thus necessitating a complete reorganization of the space. The surface finishes (floors, walls and ceilings) were to be stripped and redone. The clients also wanted to maximize on storage space, and at the same time create as much openness as possible without compromising privacy. Finally, the views, particularly those to the south and west, were to be maximized.

These stipulations were met with the architects' solution of creating three zones. The "formal" zone is that housing the living/dining room, an open kitchen, entrance and guest room; the "family" zone encompasses the den, bedrooms and children's bathroom; and, finally, the "master suite" features a study, master bedroom, bathroom and balcony.

Each zone is arranged in a unique spatial configuration generated by the program and the location/orientation of the spaces within the building. The formal zone is a grand space occupying a full third of the whole house with new windows as wide as 14 feet (4.27 m) to capture the spectacular views and natural light of the southwest corner. The family zone is organized along a translucent colored acrylic wall that brings the spaces together with the soft glow of light. The master suite is a pinwheel of volumes arranged along the windows at the northwest corner of the apartment.

Maple flooring and cabinetry tie the zones together, while each space contains its own distinguishing elements. For example, cabinetry in an amalgam of black leather, stone and glass defines the formal zone, while a maple-colored translucent wall frames the family zone, and a dramatic plaster-sculpted Venetian wall/ceiling predominates in the master suite.

These apparently monolithic and monochromatic elements, such as cabinets and built-in furniture, are assembled from different materials with mitered joints to obtain subtle changes in materials at each surface. For example, the black built-in cabinets in the living room have black leather doors, black lacquered sides, black glass at the back and a black stone top. Because the mitered joints conceal the thickness of the materials, the material differences reveal themselves only when you are next to the object - from a distance they appear monolithic.

The "formal" zone of the apartment occupies a full third of the entire apartment and features windows as wide as 14 feet (4.27 meters). The living room is furnished in built-in cabinetry with leather doors, black-lacquered sides, black glass at the back and a black stone top. These apparently disparate materials form a unified whole, due to the mitered joints between surfaces.

Each zone is arranged in a unique spatial configuration generated by the program and the location/orientation of the spaces within the building.

Cabinetry in an amalgam of black leather, stone and glass defines the formal zone, while a maple-colored translucent wall frames the family zone, and a dramatic plaster-sculpted Venetian wall/ceiling predominates in the master suite.

Michele Saee Studio

Infinite Interior-Template House

Beijing, China

Photographs: Chen Su

The design for the condominium in Phoenix City, Beijing, challenges the conventions of elemental structure and is an attempt to produce a flowing space where everyday activities take place with the least amount of resistance and clutter. The new design, conceived as a "template house", unifies the space by joining the floor, walls and ceiling into a continuous surface that accommodates the functions and technical necessities of the new living organism. The space has its own flexibility and can be modified through shifting materials, moveable partitions, and an infinite number of templates that can be customized by each tenant. This secondary skin creates an environment that shifts and changes according to the needs and wishes of the inhabitants.

The design of the house was developed in two parts: the outer container, which was the existing concrete building, and the inner container, which was the Template house. Like the body, both spaces were composed of many parts. The individual elements had to work together to ensure balance.

It all began with the idea of the template, which stemmed from the line drawings not being an accurate representation of the shapes when presented to the carpenter. Suddenly, with the line drawings, the issue became more of the nature of the lines than on what they were describing. How the line was drawn, its thickness, its errors, and so on, would become an additional determinate in the shapes rather than an actual definition. As a result of the drawing's limitations, a template was required to help move the process ahead.

The templates were constructed by the carpenters on site from the designer's drawings using a simple piece of bendable wood and a pencil. The templates were then given to the other carpenters and the process continued, and from those templates, more templates were constructed. Once the formwork had been constructed, sheathing began and the process continued. The sheets of plywood were bent on top of the frame to the shapes that the templates had defined and they were installed sheet by sheet. There was no defined construction process save for experimentation and eventually the success of one of the panels became the pattern for the rest.

Architecture:
Michele Saee

Design assistant:
Franco Rosete, Zhang Haitong

Interior designer:
Michele Saee Studio

Lighting:
Michele Saee Studio

General contractor:
Sundart, Dongguan Sundart Timber Products Co.Ltd.

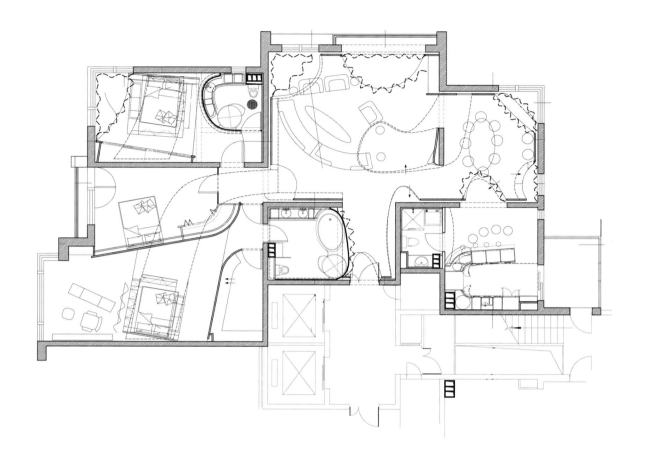

Designing and building in China was a welcoming and challenging experience for this American architect, who tried to imagine how future occupants might one day respond to this space. The design process, therefore, was eventually "surrendered to Feng Shui" as a guiding principle in achieving a sense of harmony and balance. The Ch'i, the cosmic breath, the human spirit, is that which determines our movements, our actions; Feng Shui is the rule of the Ch'i.

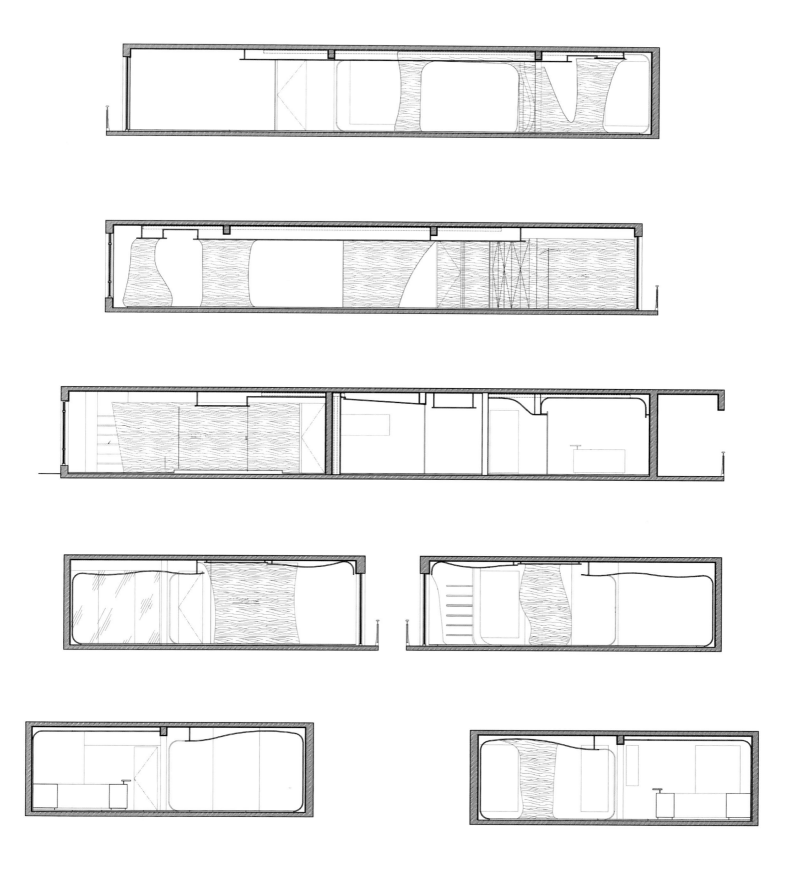

179

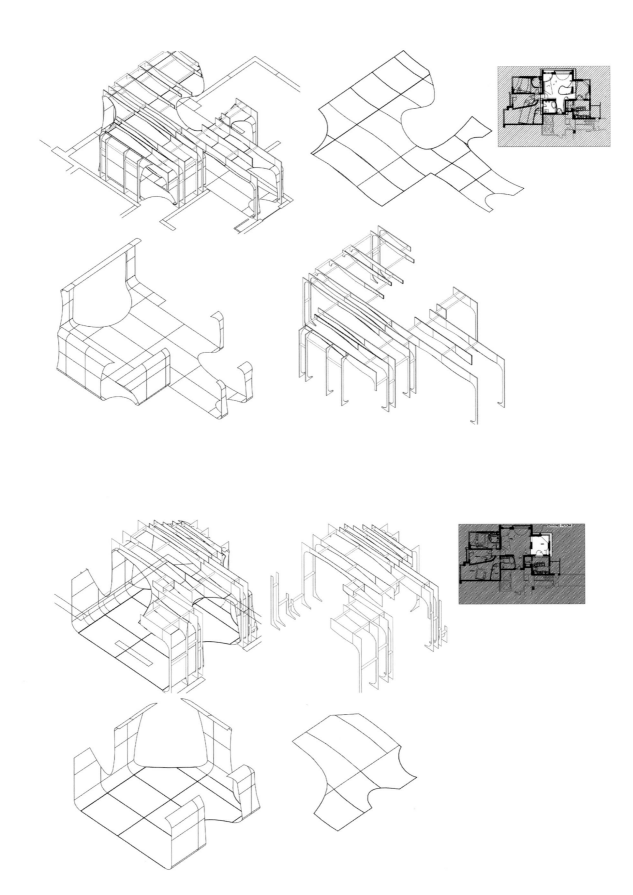

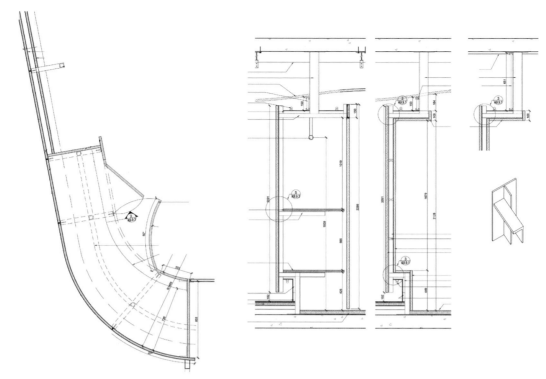

The project is one container within another; the secondary skin embodies the idea of the vessel. The design of the Template House is an experiment in whether the distinctly separate elements that work together to construct the space can be utilized in such a way that a sense of unity is achieved outside the ceiling, walls and floor combinations that normally speak of reliance upon one another, while having separate roles in the space.

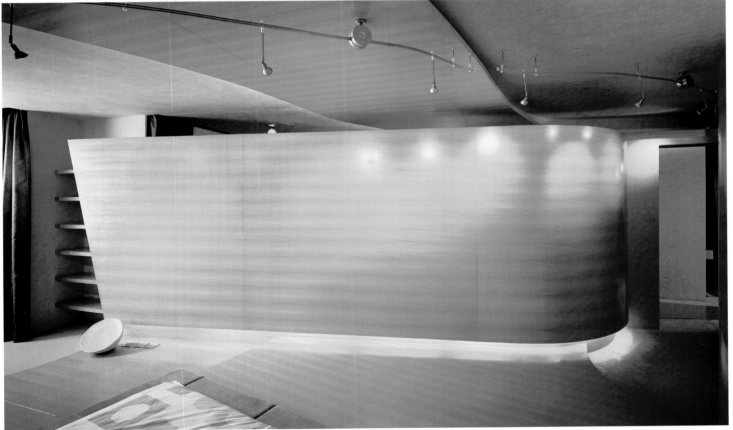

Neeson Murcutt Architects

Whale Beach House

Sydney, Australia

Photographs: Brett Boardman Photography

Whale Beach House is located in the southeast fold of a steep, thickly vegetated hillside, below a towering escarpment and between the beach and the main road. The positioning of the house is derived from a pragmatic mapping of adjacent building alignments, northpoint, neighbors' view lines and required setbacks. These invisible lines establish the oblique geometries that characterize the plan.

The house is a multi-generational family weekender organized over three levels that terrace with the slope – children and grandparents on the lower level, main living areas on the mid level and parents 'secret' timber cabin on top. The plan is stratified, each level deliberately distinct from the other with internal stairs that are virtually hidden. Whilst the ceiling of each level is constant, the floors are stepped or 'topographic'.

The project explores proximity and distance, invoking the special dualities of the site – the rocky outcrops and native forest behind are given equal consideration to the front coastal panorama. Each room is considered almost autonomously, coordinated with the site and view. The experience of the house is cinematic, with the view partitioned so that it becomes particular to each room – the horizon from the kitchen, the headland from the living room, the escarpment from the main entry, the rainforest at the back door. An array of opening types assists the orchestration – solid timber shutters that reveal the view when open, sashes that completely disappear, windows that capture the view within a sheet of fixed glass and strategic skylights for light without view. These strategies generate a spatial richness experienced as 'surprise'.

Like its neighbors the house is elevated above the street, providing a degree of privacy. It is strongly articulated with upper levels clad in recycled timber that will darken in time to camouflage against the backdrop of the scarp. A void through the center of the lower masonry level creates a view through to the garden. The native landscape is metaphorically drawn through this void connecting with neighboring gardens across the front. Careful collaboration between the landscape architect, hydraulic engineer, ecologist and builder allowed the waterway on the northeast side of the building to be restored, resisting the council's attempts to create a storm water easement and instead enriching the landscape setting. The house and landscape are integral. Outdoor living spaces correspond with each level of the house and are equally varied.

The project demonstrates a holistic approach to sustainability through: solar orientation, natural light, ventilation, efficient internal heating, material choices, water collection, locally indigenous plantings and the compact pool.

Architecture:
Neeson Murcutt Architects
Principal architects:
Rachel Neeson, Nicholas Murcutt
Project team:
Andrew Burns, Amelia Holiday, Jeff Morgan, Sean Choo, David Coleborne
Contractor:
Coddington Constructions Pty Ltd
Landscape architect:
Sue Barnsley Design
Structural engineer:
Tihanyi Consulting Engineers

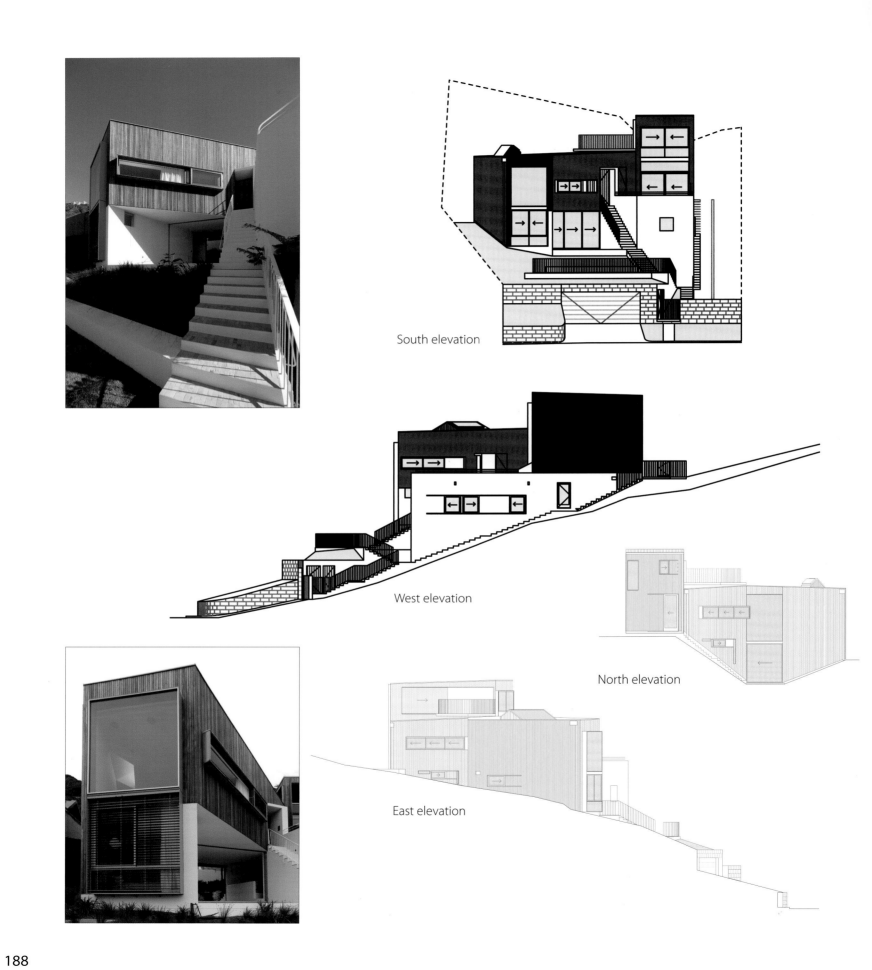

South elevation

West elevation

North elevation

East elevation

LEVEL 3

1. Main bedroom
2. Deck
3. Ensuite
4. WC
5. Roof
6. Rainforest garden

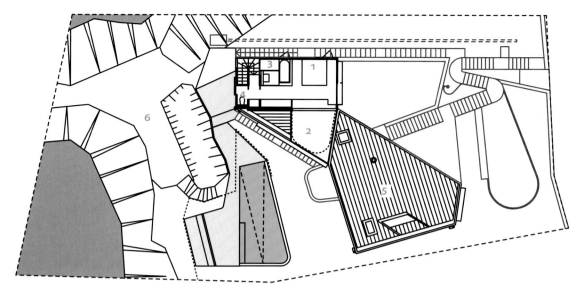

LEVEL 2

7. Entry
8. Lounge
9. Fireplace
10. WC
11. Dining room
12. Dining terrace
13. Kitchen
14. Kitchen terrace
15. Pool terrace
16. Pool
17. Filed seat
18. Graded garden gully

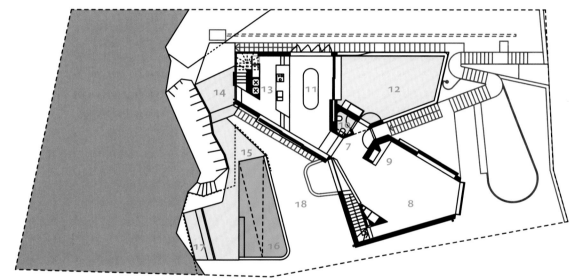

LEVEL 1

19. Lawn terrace
20. Outdoor shower
21. Inclinator
22. Playroom terrace
23. Playroom
24. Guest bedroom
25. Ensuite
26. TV nook
27. Bedroom
28. Bathroom
29. WC
30. Laundry
31. Services

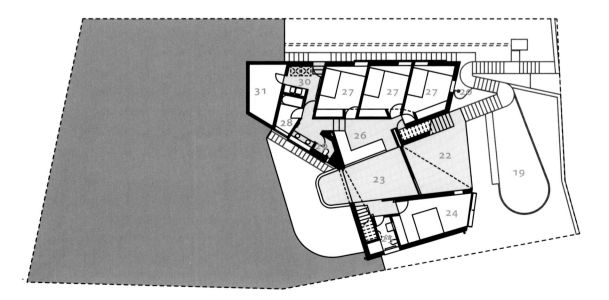

A void through the center of the lower masonry level creates a view through to the garden. The native landscape is metaphorically drawn through this void connecting with neighboring gardens across the front.

Terrelonge

Wedge Profile

Toronto, Canada

Photographs: Rico Bella

Architecture:
Terrelonge
Master builder:
Bob Mitchel

The Wedge gallery was a commission which called for two separate but complimentary spaces with areas that flowed into one another. The space doubles as an art gallery and a loft. The upper area contains the private space: the bedroom and a bathroom. The lower level is a multi-functional public space which houses a spare room, a kitchen, a living room/entertainment area and the Wedge Gallery. Presented with a long narrow interior between demising walls, some 140 sqm in area, the architects decided to play with generatin gtensions within the space by applying techniques from graphic design. The client's love of music and art is expressed in the fixtures, rooms and storage cabinets that Terrelonge created. To store the client's 3,000+ CDs, the architects created tall 6 x 3 ft units to house the collection, with an interior "closet" that houses stereo equipment. The fireplace and white wall spaces provide clean surfaces on which to display the artworks. The finishing materials used include sandblasted glass, matt aluminum, brushed stainless steel and poured concrete.

The overall look is comfortable, inviting, complex yet simple. With apartment fulfils many functions in one: it is at once a private space, a public space, a space for entertaining and for low key activities.

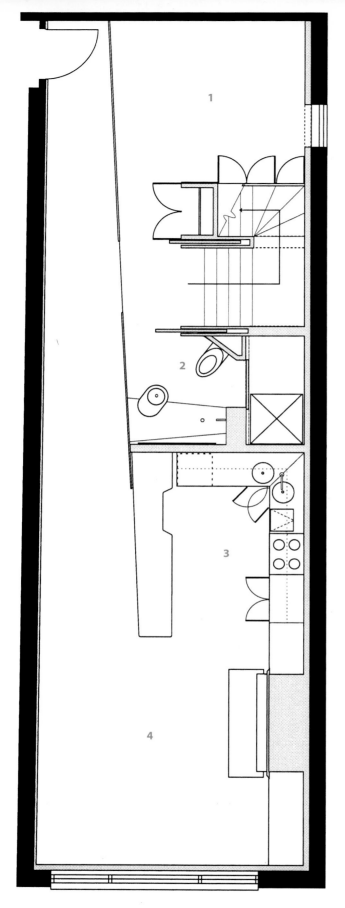

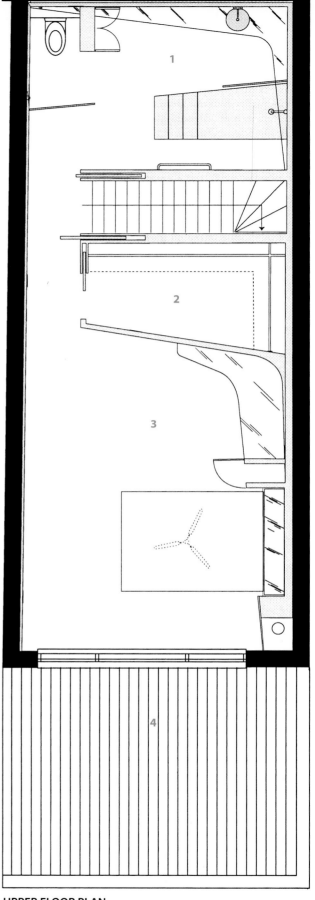

MAIN FLOOR PLAN

1. Room
2. Bathroom
3. Kitchen
4. Living room

UPPER FLOOR PLAN

1. Bathroom
2. Dressing room
3. Room
4. Deck

198

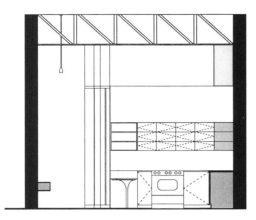

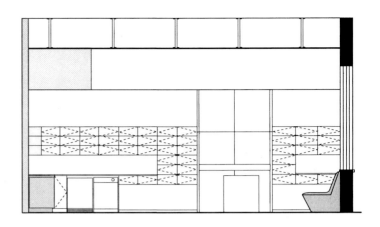

Kitchen sections

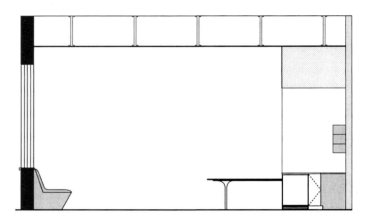

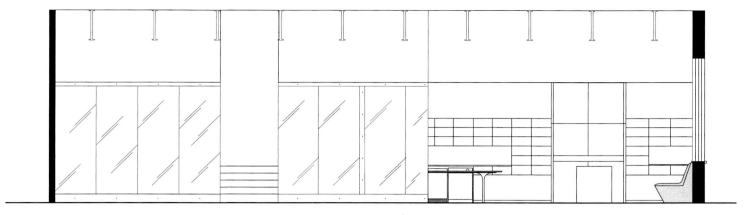

Glass wall elevation

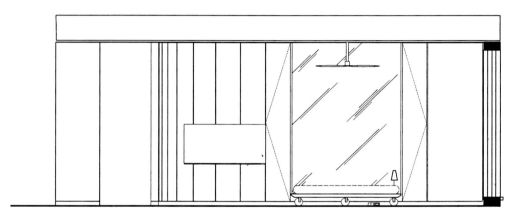

Bedroom elevation

The design concept of the dwelling/gallery was based on spatial criteria linked to the interpretation of the inhabitable space according to space-time and functional coordinates. The different atmospheres therefore have no specific definition and can adapt to changing uses.

SAMARK
Arkitektur & Design AB

Turning Torso Apartments

Malmö, Sweden

Photographs: James Silverman

This building was designed as a sculptural landmark, thus calling for an ambitious interior that would live up to its remarkable exterior. The very shape of the building presented as many difficulties as it did unique opportunities. For example, the number of doors leading from the staircase core / elevator shaft as well as the thickness of the concrete core brought with them certain prerequisites and obstacles.

On the other hand, the plan enabled four excellent "living room positions" per floor - rooms spanning corners or spaces placed along the fully glazed façade. The shape of the plan also naturally inspired rather large apartments in relation to the number of rooms, since connecting partitions facing the leaning façade had to be avoided.

The aim was to create large living rooms that would be directly linked to partly open kitchens. The entryways are also open, generously proportioned spaces, whose floors are clad in polished Swedish limestone, a material also used on all of the window sills along the façades.

In most of the large apartments the bedrooms have been separated from the more "public" areas, which are constituted by the entrance hall, living room, dining area and kitchen. Oiled oak is the flooring used in all other areas, except the bathrooms.

Massive full-height doors in light glazed oak and sliding doors close off the bedrooms and bathrooms in an otherwise very open floor plan. Accentuated architrave and trim complements the doors at floor height. All wardrobes have been completely built into the walls.

The bathrooms have been fully tiled in a small clinker on the floors and a somewhat larger tile on the walls. The countertops in the bathrooms and kitchens are available in three varieties of granite and one of the walls in the kitchen is clad in ceramic tiling. The cupboards, which come in a range of materials to choose from, such as light glazed oak, white glossy laminate or alu-minum with oak trimmings, have been custom designed for the project.

The ceilings throughout are smooth and white and the ceiling height in the living room is raised to slightly more than 2,700 mm. The kitchens, bathrooms, toilets and laundry rooms are supplied with recessed spotlights.

Architecture:
SAMARK
Arkitektur & Design AB

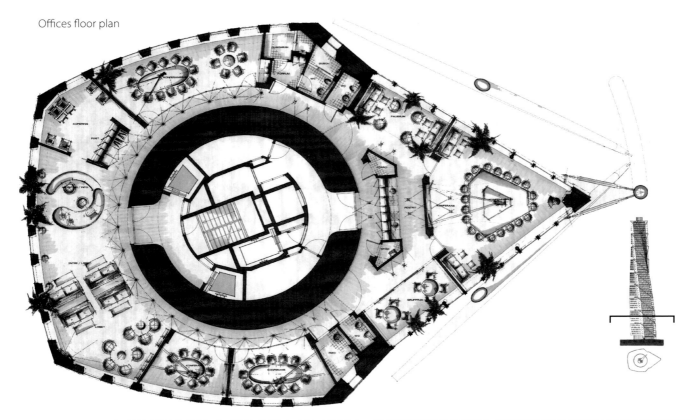

Offices floor plan

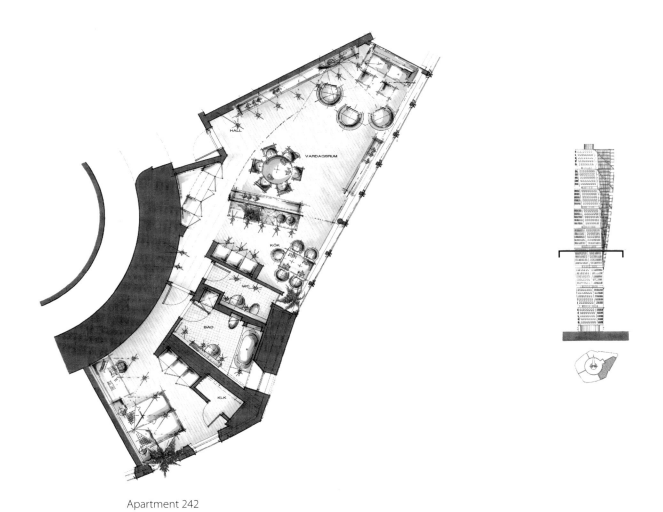

Apartment 242

Apartment 243

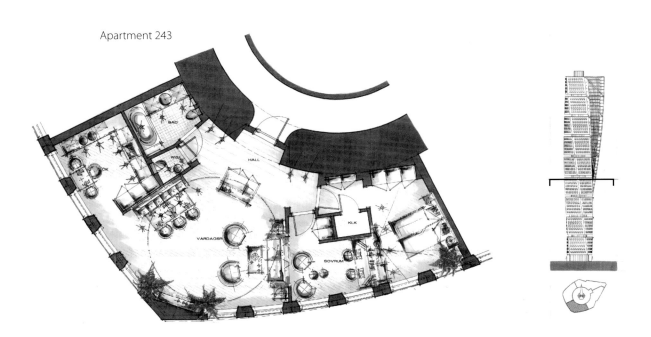

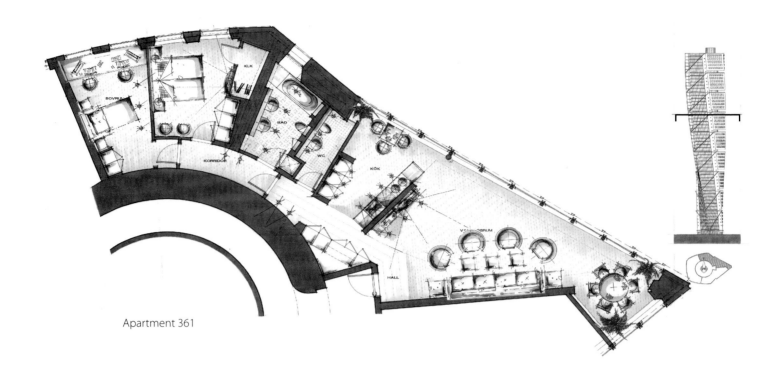

Apartment 361

Apartment 511

The aim was to create large living rooms that would be directly linked to partly open kitchens. The entryways are also open, generously proportioned spaces, whose floors are clad in polished Swedish limestone, a material also used on all of the window sills along the façades.

Messana O'Rorke Architects

The Pent Tank House

New York, USA   **Photographs:** Elizabeth Felicella

The project involved the renovation of an existing loft apartment and the development of an existing sprinkler tank house into an urban retreat.

The apartment's simple layout was maintained, but reconfigured so that the bedrooms had individual access to a shared bathroom rather than it being accessed from the living space, (a powder room in the entry way meant that guests would not need to access the bathroom). The sky lit bathroom doubled in size and was developed to have a serene spa like quality, with a continuous stone floor, polished waterproof plaster walls, and clear glass shower enclosure. In the living room and bedrooms new storage was introduced at every possible point behind hidden flush lacquer panels. The kitchen was resurfaced and the maple wood floors were lightened and refinished. A custom stainless steel spiral stair replaced an ugly painted steel stair with wood treads. The client anticipated that a new stair would encourage him to ascend more frequently to his roof deck and Tank House.

A tree house perched high in a city of towers and skyscrapers. The tank house was conceived as the quintessential retreat, a room for reading, relaxing and listening to music.

The refurbished roof deck was given new trees and landscape; it had existed for a number of years, over-shadowed by a looming tar covered rotunda occupied by an enormous cast iron sprinkler tank. The removal of this tank and the introduction of a new structural frame to support the crumbing terracotta walls of the rotunda were essential difficulties of this project. The building was shored-up by an external wood frame and the tank was slowly cut into manageable pieces with blowtorches. Once removed the true proportions of the internal space were revealed and it was tempting to leave it as a raw industrial space, but the program requirements and in particular the need for the room to be usable year round meant moving forward as planned.

A twelve-foot tall window was cut into the east side of the space and the new window looked out onto the roof deck plantings. A circular skylight was introduced into center, casting an ethereal light into the space. The floor of maple matched the apartment and was segmented into removable panels providing access to storage space below.

Architecture:
Messana O'Rorke Architects

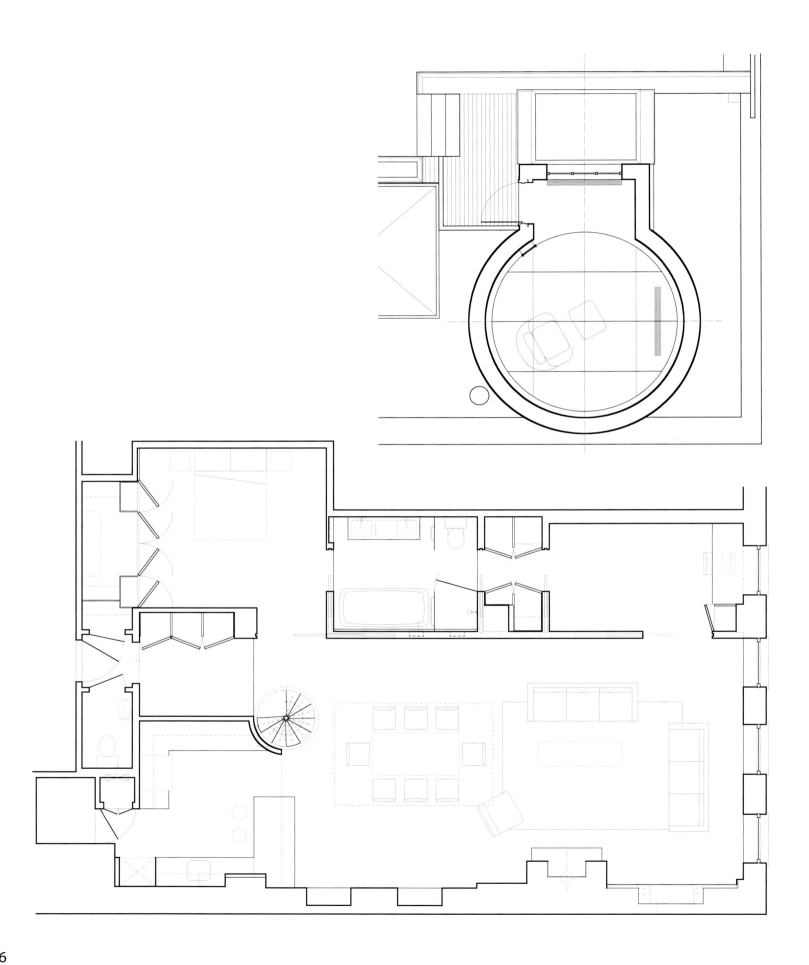

216

The sky lit bathroom doubled in size and was developed to have a serene spa like quality, with a continuous stone floor, polished waterproof plaster walls, and clear glass shower enclosure. In the living room and bedrooms new storage was introduced at every possible point behind hidden flush lacquer panels.

Gaëlle Hamonic &
Jean-Christophe Masson

House in a garage Abbadie

Paris, France   **Photographs:** Hervé Abbadie / Hamonic + Masson Architectes

When a couple with children who appreciate spaciousness and contemporary design as much as they abhor pattern book suburban houses decided to free themselves from the corset of a traditional Parisian apartment building, they decided to commission an architect to build them a custom-designed home. With the same boldness they offered the project to young designers. The success of a project is often a question of confidence.

The chain that was established in the course of this project between the clients, the architect and the contractor is a perfect illustration of this principle. From the first sketch to handover of the finished house took just one year. The dedication of the architects to the project was proportional to the confidence that the clients placed in them.

And this is how an old shell opening onto a passage on the outskirts of the old quarter of Paris became their ideal house. The project was not, strictly speaking, a renovation, but rather a more radical intervention, a way of making full use of the plot.

Two different environments are woven together: on the passage side, the old houses are preserved, with their roofing and their loft. In the heart of the block, in place of the old hangar, the fluid space of the new intervention expands.

The house takes the old dimensions of the shell (192 sqm floor space, 6 m height to the base of the roof), crossed by a courtyard (3 m x 6 m). The 18 sqm of space planted with bamboo becomes a garden, a source of light and garden views for all the rooms.

Preserving its original character, the street façade is practically unaltered. This choice of discretion and respect for the surrounding fabric helped the inhabitants of this modest dead-end passageway in old Paris to accept the project.

On crossing the threshold, the visitor is drawn inwards towards a large, extremely open volume (the living room), which opens onto the court. The scenario of daily life is thus discovered. The different spaces are linked by the interplay of light and the contrast of volumes. No doors, no obstacles. Transitions take the form of delicate filters: a bamboo hedge in the courtyard, a set of transparent or translucent polycarbonate screens to separate off the kitchen, dining area, lounge and offices.

Architecture:
Gaëlle Hamonic & Jean-Christophe Masson

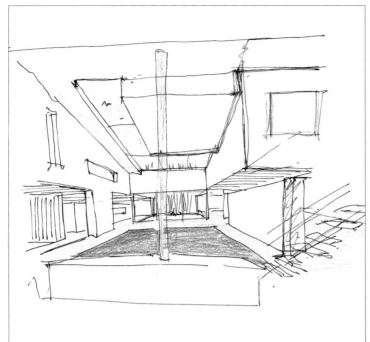

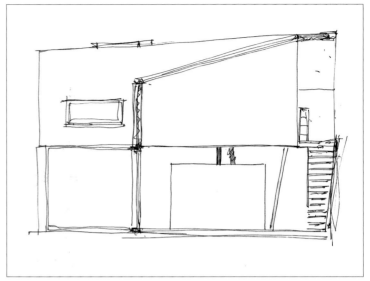

In fitting out the dwelling the architects avoided any mannerism in the materials, using only what was essential for the house to breathe: a metal structure, white or colored partitions, transparencies.

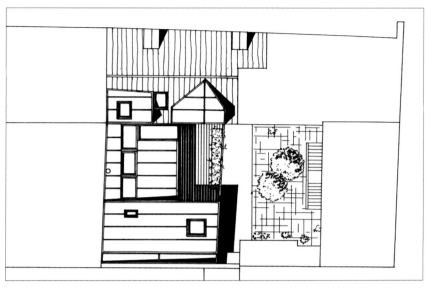

Children live on the passage side, in the loft. They have their own staircase and bathroom. At the end of the plot, the parents' room hangs suspended and under the Parisian sky.

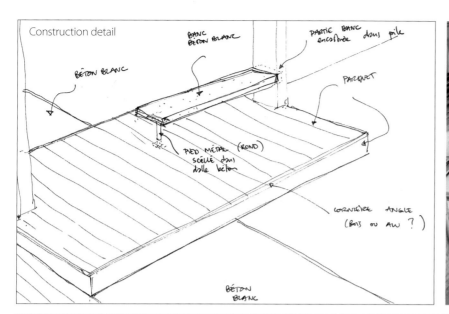

Construction detail

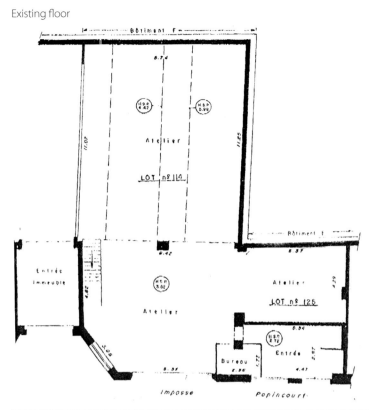

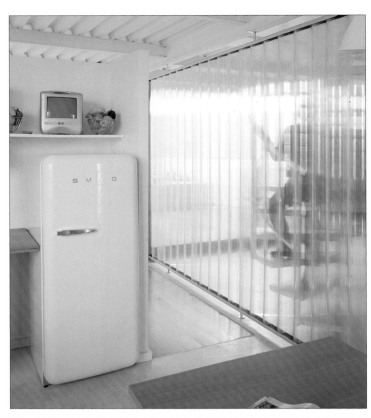

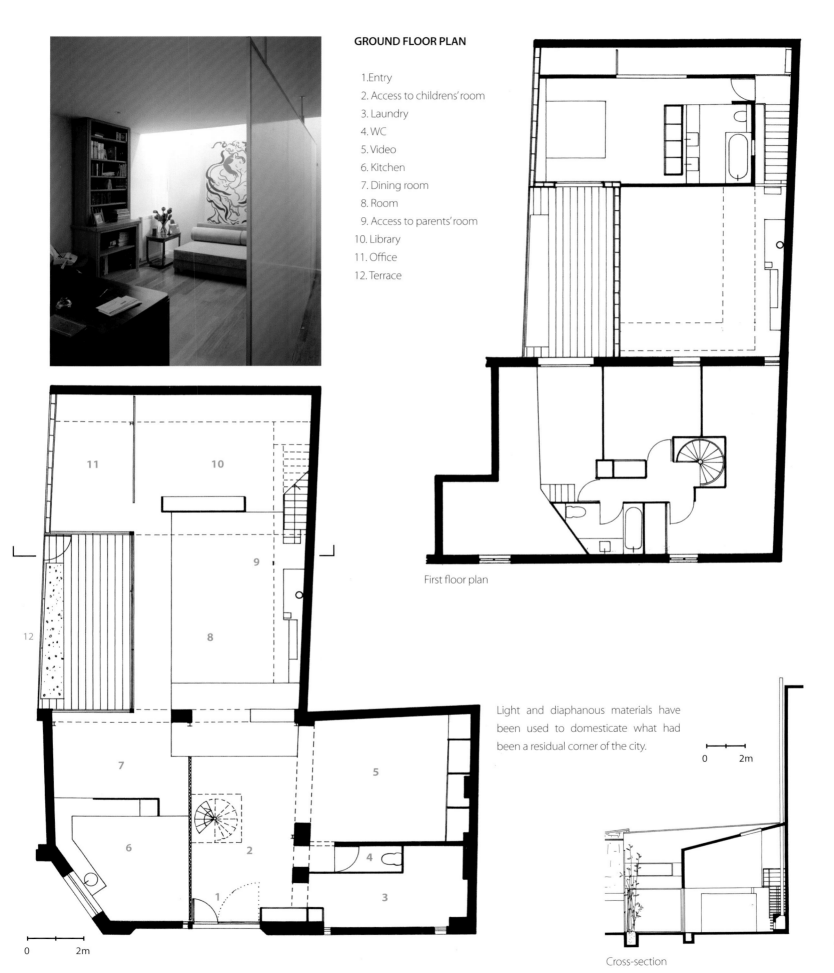

GROUND FLOOR PLAN

1. Entry
2. Access to childrens' room
3. Laundry
4. WC
5. Video
6. Kitchen
7. Dining room
8. Room
9. Access to parents' room
10. Library
11. Office
12. Terrace

First floor plan

Light and diaphanous materials have been used to domesticate what had been a residual corner of the city.

0   2m

Cross-section

Peter Hulting Architect
Meter Arkitektur

Guest Appearance

Gothenburg, Sweden

Photographs: James Silverman

Architecture:
Peter Hulting Architect
Meter Arkitektur

When Swedish architect Peter Hulting was asked to transform this old farm site into a couple's new home, he immediately saw the potential to create an unpretentious, sensitive space with the ability to connect both to its immediate surroundings and the neighboring open landscape. Specific only in their demands for a concrete floor and clay roof tiles, quality craftsmanship and simplicity were key to the couple's vision of "a house that could age with dignity".

Walking into this small summer house situated on Sweden's west coast peninsula, you are immediately struck by a sense of space that belies its 538 square feet (50 sq m) of floor space. Everything from the furniture to the lighting has been designed to enhance the building's shape and size - from the elongated Japanese-style table and benches, to the long steel-pipe chimney that guides the eye upwards from the open fire to the wooden ceiling.

A combination of wood, concrete and plaster creates a range of tactile surfaces that compare and contrast in equal measure. The smooth concrete floor incorporates the water-carried heating system, while the use of sawed larch tree for the exterior walls and reclaimed clay tiles on the roof allow the building to sit perfectly within this picturesque setting.

In order to maximize on the available space, Hulting opted for an open plan design. By creating a large glass frontage overlooking the south-facing landscape, sliding doors define the inner space when required, while at the same time ensuring the interior of the guesthouse remains cool in the summer. Creating compact solutions in such a reduced space was central to the design concept; this was achieved, in part, by allowing the dividing walls to work like large pieces of furniture within the main space. Towards one end a wardrobe doubles as a wall divider, separating the sleeping area from the rest of the house. The reverse of this wardrobe doubles as a set of bookshelves at the foot of the bed. There is also space for two loft beds here, while the simple design of Ulf Scherlin's "Birå 4" cupboard ensures that any clutter is neatly stored away out of sight.

To the left of the bedroom, two sliding doors conceal the toilet and shower areas. The floors, tiled in Portuguese stone, offset standard white tiles that have been 'brick-mounted' and finished with a dark gray grout.

The kitchen sits in a semi-recess, cleverly defining its parameters without encroaching on the open-plan design of the overall space. The stainless steel of the kitchen contrasts beautifully with brightly colored handmade Portuguese tiles.

The shape of the dining table and benches add to the sense of space. Large sliding glass doors capitalize on the view and provide easy access to the exterior deck.

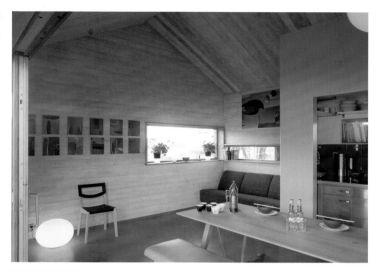

Non Kitch Group bvba

Architecture and lifestyle

Koksijde, Belgium

Photographs: Jan Verlinde

Architecture:
Non Kitch Group bvba

Transforming an old canning factory in Bruges into an impressive loft dwelling was a great challenge with endless attractive possibilities for the designers. One of the most significant features of this scheme by architect Linda Arschoot and designer William Sweetlove, the creators of the Non Kitch Group, was the remodeled roof. It was formed by a lattice structure with a dog-tooth profile supporting a conventional roof. They decided to replace the north sides of each of the parallel roofs with a glazed surface. These skylights greatly increase the natural lighting in the whole dwelling, as in many museums or art galleries. Due to the considerable height of the building (6 m, 20 ft), this intervention also meant that the interior was almost converted into an outside piazza. A large, full-height room open to the exterior occupies the center of the space and is surrounded by a mezzanine that houses the kitchen, the dining room, the bar and the television room. Under this mezzanine, three steps below the level of the living room are the billiards room, the bedroom, the dressing room, the gym and the bathroom that gives directly onto the small garden. The covered pool is located on one side of this exterior space, with an elegant decoration of vertical mosaic strips. An outdoors area also provides better views and enhances the dimensions of the space.

The conservation of the industrial aspect of the building is shown through the use of metal doors, the heating pipes, the separate kitchen, the galvanized iron staircase and the view of the old factory chimney through the parallel skylights of the roof. In opposition to the asceticism of minimalist interiors, the Non Kitch Group consider themselves to be the heirs of the humor and the colorist aesthetics of the Memphis group. One of the premises of this scheme was to generate an appropriate space for viewing the works of art of the private collection of the owners. The furniture is a forceful presence in this dwelling. Designed by Ettore Sottsass, Philippe Starck, Boris Spiek, Jean Nouvel, Norman Foster and the architects themselves, it seems to be made to measure for this spacious loft.

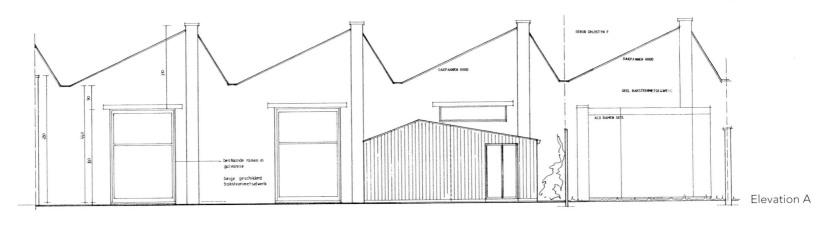

Elevation A

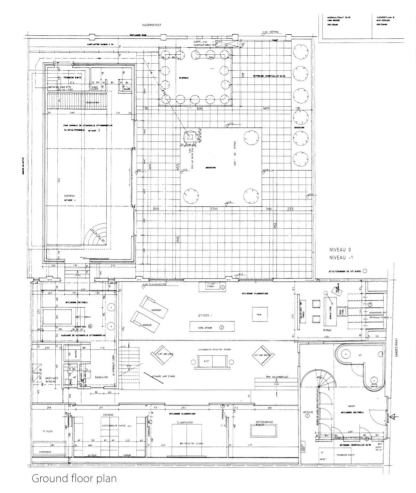

Ground floor plan

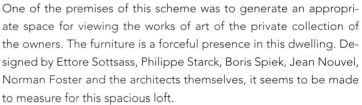

One of the premises of this scheme was to generate an appropriate space for viewing the works of art of the private collection of the owners. The furniture is a forceful presence in this dwelling. Designed by Ettore Sottsass, Philippe Starck, Boris Spiek, Jean Nouvel, Norman Foster and the architects themselves, it seems to be made to measure for this spacious loft.

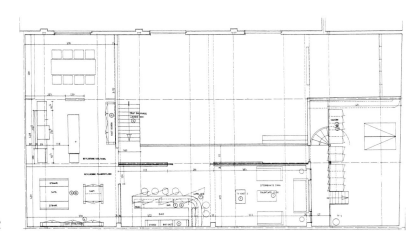

Levels 1 and 2

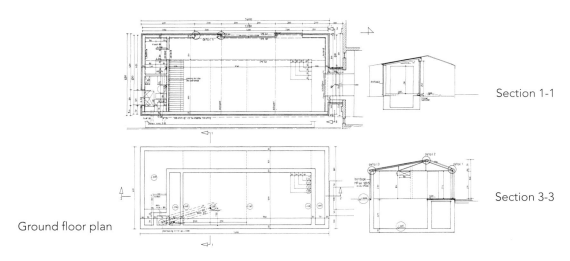

Section 1-1

Ground floor plan

Section 3-3

The metal elements used throughout the loft contribute an industrial air that recalls the former use of the building. The central location of the kitchen and the simple forms are a clear example of the emotions and contrasts sought by the Non Kitch Group.

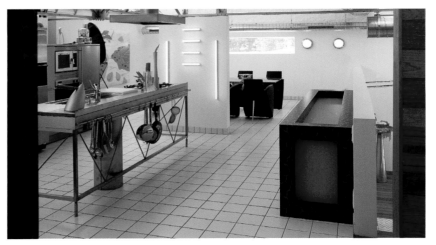

Johanna Grawunder

Beach House in Milan

Milan, Italy   **Photographs:** Santi Caleca

The design approach for the interior of this beach house was to look for the "essence" of the existing open space and respect it as much as possible.

This was achieved by painting the existing concrete structure matt black in order to highlight it, so that the structure itself became the most striking element of the loft. The emphasis was on creating an easy and elegant environment, using mainly inexpensive materials, and leaving different areas as open as possible while allowing the structure to define the space.

The few volumes in the space arose from the need for some private areas within this very strong cultural grid. In order to respect the mainly post and beam construction, the few walls that where required were designed to look like separate volumes, huddling under the structural grid.

Paint was used to define the space and create different effects, black for the structural grid, light blue for the ceiling, and different shades of green and gray for the volumes. The finishes and furniture were carefully chosen to create an environment where various levels of refinement could comfortably coexist - a few custom designed pieces mixed with other simple and inexpensive or industrial-style furniture. The house consists of a master bedroom and bathroom, a simple kitchen and an open plan living area. Sliding doors separate the bedroom from the main room, so that it can be open to the rest of the house. The emphasis is on maximum flexibility of use and movement through the space.

Architecture:
Johanna Grawunder

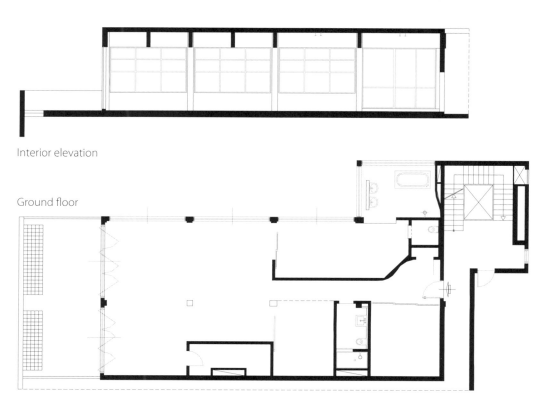

Interior elevation

Ground floor

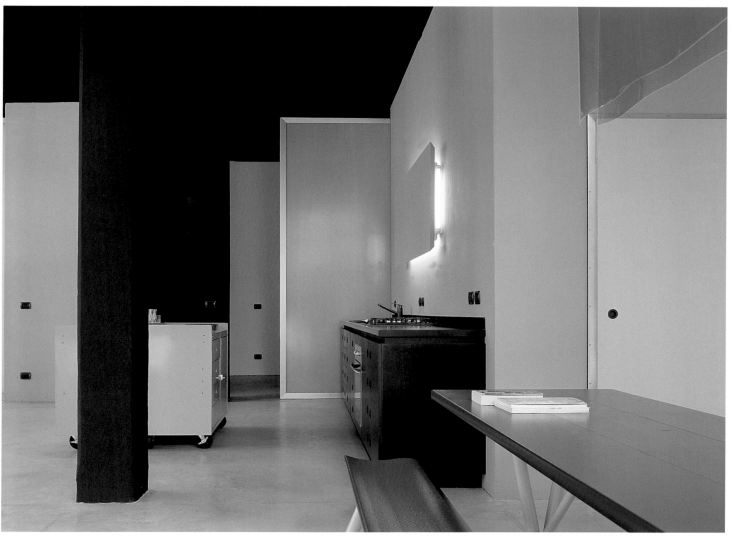

Combarel & Marrec

Fiat Loft

Paris, France

Photographs: Benoît Fougeirol

Architecture:
Combarel & Marrec

The site for the project is the back end of a Parisian block mainly occupied by workshops. The building sits on what used to be a light-filled backyard which was gradually filled in with built structures. Subsequently, the building itself is wedged in tightly among other buildings that are mostly higher than it. Bringing light into the house, therefore, became a central concern in the new design.

The volume to be restructured was composed of three different spaces: the covered backyard (a makeshift glass roof had been put in place at some point), the basement and a spare room located in the raised ground floor, which was not accessible from the building's stairwell.

The only way of ensuring a modicum of natural light in this hemmed in site was via a glass roof. The challenge and aim therefore became applying the same qualities and status of a conventional façade to a horizontal plane, which also had to bear certain necessary characteristics of ceiling and roof.

The roof and all its components are at the service of the views and natural light. The envelope has been conceived as a sort of periscope which goes in search of fragments of the sky and the surrounding built landscape, bringing them back down into the apartment for the enjoyment of its inhabitants. The light and environment are thereby broken up and re-assembled into a composed image. The glass roof becomes an oversized kaleidoscope offering a shifting, fragmented image of the surroundings. An exterior volume - the courtyard - has been set up in the interior of the layout and capped by the glass roof as an inversion of the sheltered surfaces.

The entire apartment is assembled around this inverted room, which is framed with floor-to-ceiling sliding glass panels that allow a complete reorganization of the interior space, depending on how much intimacy is desired.

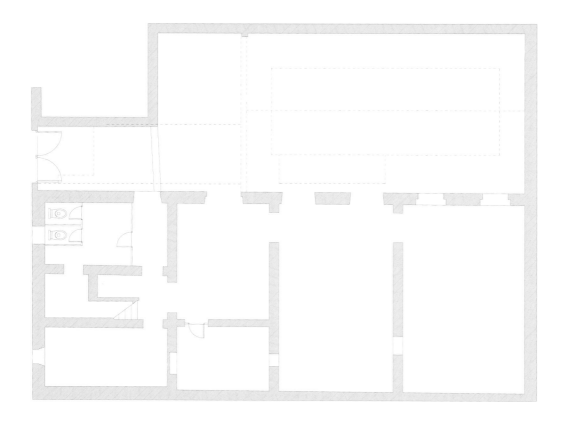

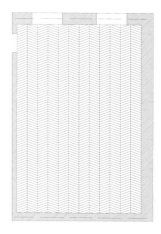

The building occupies what used to be a light-filled courtyard which has been filled in with built structures over the years and, consequently, is hemmed in by taller buildings. Since a conventional façade was out of the question, the challenge was to treat a horizontal plane both as roof and façade.

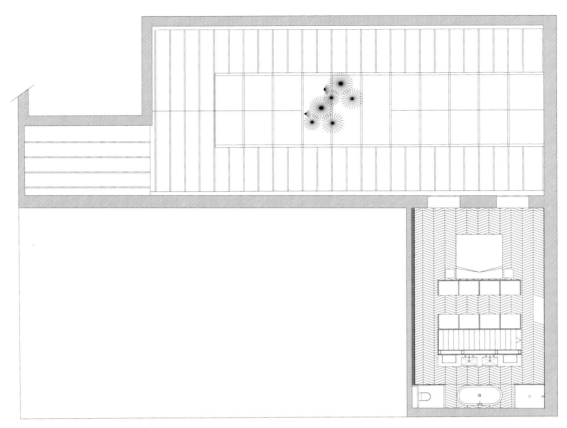

Ground floor plan

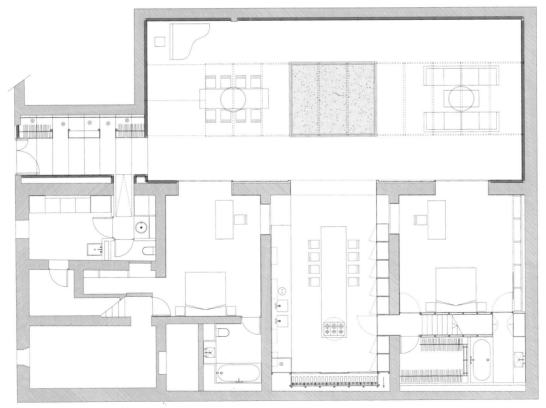

First floor plan

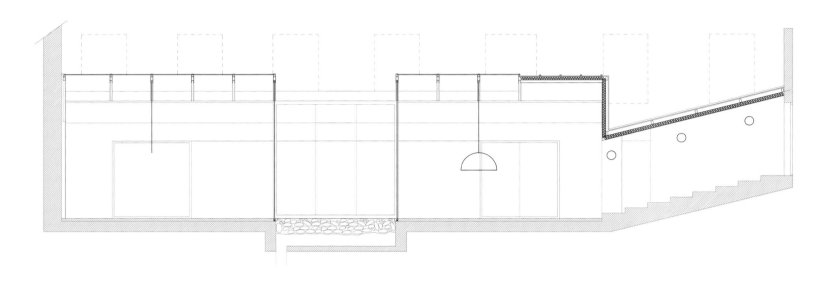

Longitudinal section

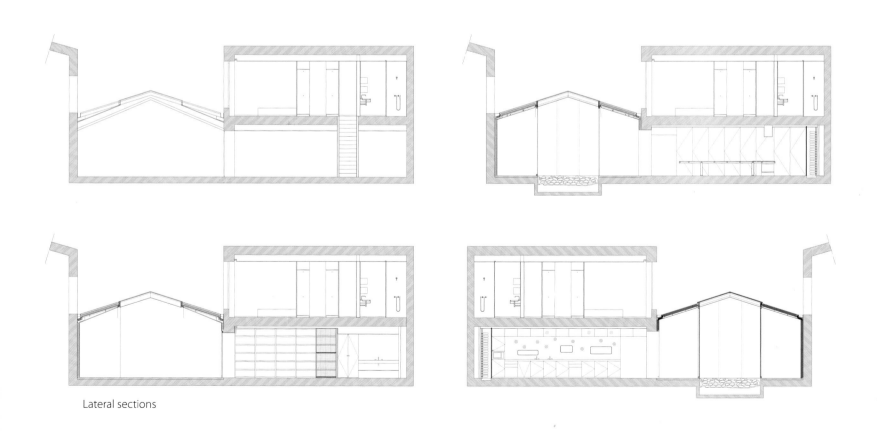

Lateral sections

Christian Pottgiesser

House in Rue Galvani

Paris, France   **Photographs:** Gert von Bassewitz & Pascale Thomas

The project for this house, designed to accommodate seven people, is the result of the extension of a private house located at the rear of a narrow 140 sqm (1,500 sqft) site. The brief specified maintaining the entire garden, while also allowing a new structure to be built on the site. This apparent paradox became the key to the project. Apart from the requirements of the client, an existing Japanese ailanthus and lime tree were protected by the Department of Parks and Gardens, making it virtually impossible to build on the perimeter of the site adjacent to the street. The architects also had to respect an early twentieth century regulation banning buildings of more than one story in the area, as well as trying not to obstruct views to the existing building.

The stone used for the façade is from the Parisian basin, the same as the stone used in the neighboring buildings. The walls, structural elements, floors and slab were built on-site using reinforced concrete. The principal walls of the house are solid stone and plywood, with a projected plaster finish. The stairs and windows, the sliding doors and the garage door are made from solid untreated iroko wood, and waxed teakwood is used for the parquet floors. Railway beams, pebbles and stone masonry are used in the garden.

Architecture:
Christian Pottgiesser

The main structuring element for the building is an irregular surface raised about 1.2 m (3.9 ft) off street level. A reinforced concrete slab rests at this level, its volume and width changing as other elements cross it or in response to circulation, lighting and layout requirements.

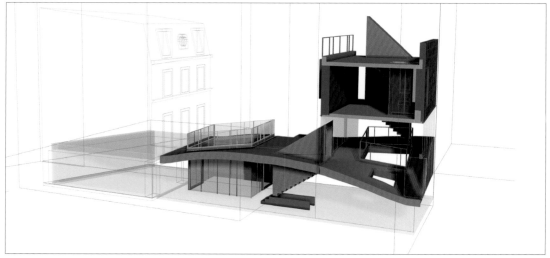

The brief specified that the entire garden had to be maintained, while also allowing a new structure to be built on the site. This apparent paradox became the key to the project. The actual house is located on the lower level, with the garden on the upper level. A car can be parked in the space created by the raised slab.

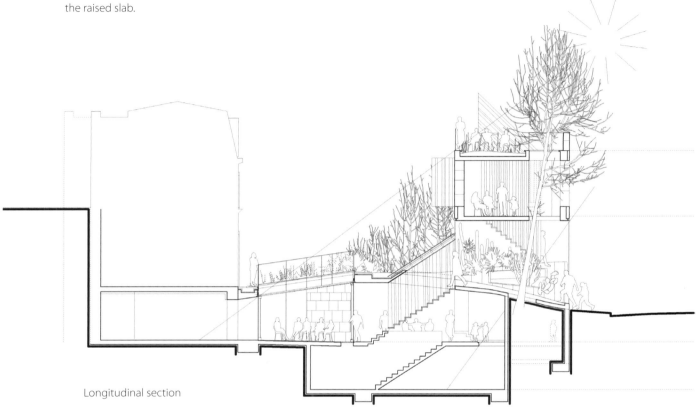

Longitudinal section

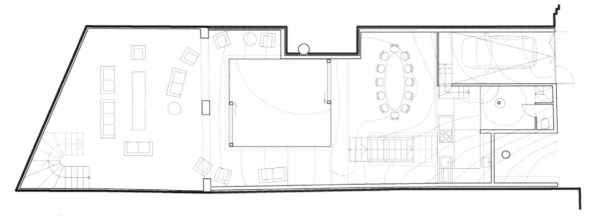

Ground floor plan

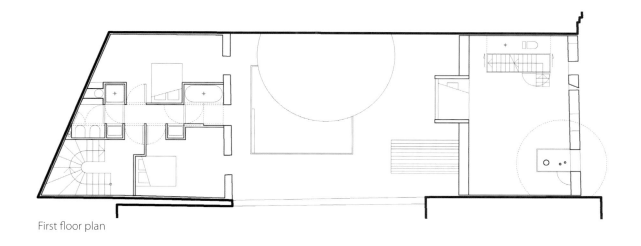

First floor plan

Architecture W

M-House

Nagoya, Japan

Photographs: Andy Boone

Architecture:
Architecture W

The site, located in one of Nagoya's more attractive residential neighborhoods, drops 7 meters (23 ft) down and with only 2.5 meters (8.2 ft) of dead end street access was considered "unbuildable". M-House addresses these conditions and provides for the simple, modern lifestyle of the American owner/architect and his family.

This 4 level project (half basement, entry level, 2nd floor, & roof deck) is more complex than it appears. Beyond the challenge of the site, the house is planned for a multi generational/multi national family, while securing precious views, sunlight, and breeze within a traditionally cramped Japanese neighborhood. The difficult site was in fact the property's redeeming feature – its inspiring location at the edge of a cliff overlooking northern Nagoya.

At the lowest level, the structure ties into additional retaining walls to carve out an apartment that is a modern twist of the Japanese notion of looking after one's parents as they get old. Instead of being integrated into the house, the apartment has its own kitchen, bathroom and access, via an exterior stair, so the client's in-laws can have their privacy while they enjoy the benefits of the site, and interact with their grandchildren in the garden space that fronts the entire apartment.

At entry level there is space for parking and turning the cars, a hallway into the house, bedrooms and the main bathing area. Here the structure supports the 2 steel trusses that cantilever the remainder of the house over the car port, to free the access of obstructions. A small pool situated under the cantilever reflects sunlight into the bathing area, where only a glass wall separates this center of Japanese family life – complete with its wooden soaking bath -from the entry area.

Besides a pantry/guest bath in the southwest corner, the top level of the house is a single open space that provides the main living area. The steel trusses that allow for the 5+ meter (16 + ft) cantilever are buried behind 2 walls of storage and kitchen cabinetry, allowing the remaining 2 sides of the steel box –north and south – to consist of glass walls that slide away for the entire room to become a terrace, from which to enjoy the spectacular view and pleasant breeze. A roof deck tops the house with another large outdoor gathering space, for entertaining.

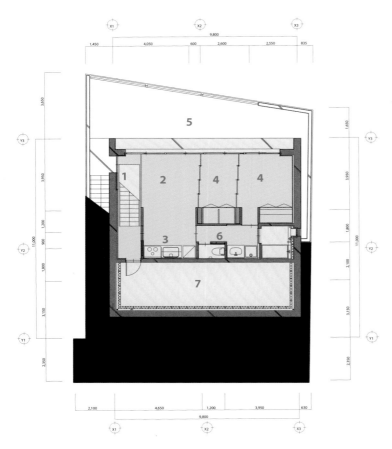

Basement plan

A structural system of reinforced concrete, concrete incased steel, and a pair of 3 meter (9.8 ft) tall steel trusses – all running inside the east and west walls of the house - allow the design to confront the site conditions, leaving the north and south elevations for sliding glass walls that capture the charm of this location: the view, the light and the breeze.

1. Entrance
2. Living – dining
3. Kitchen
4. Bedroom
5. Backyard
6. Bathroom
7. Storage
8. Closet
9. Parking
10. Pond
11. Guest room

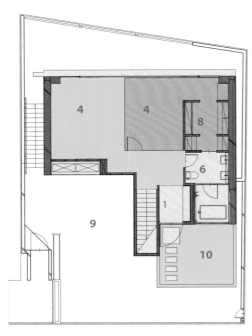

Ground floor plan

First floor plan

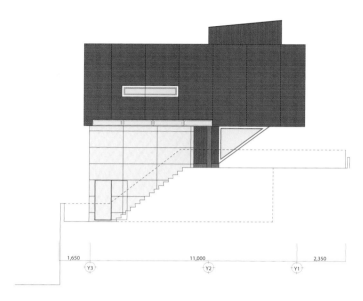

West elevation

1,650 Y3   11,000 Y2   2,350 Y1

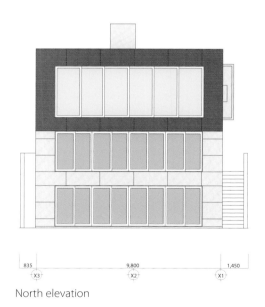

835 X3   9,800 X2   1,450 X1

North elevation

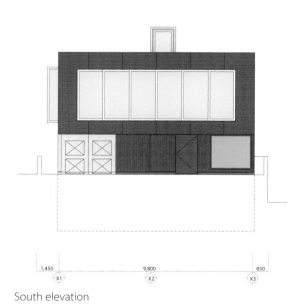

1,450 X1   9,800 X2   850 X3

South elevation

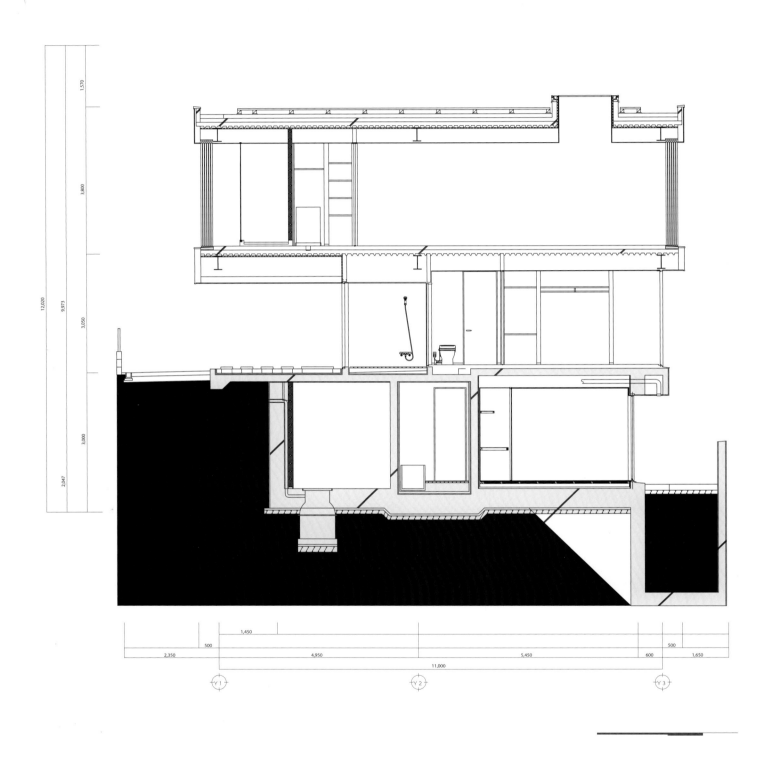

The main stair well, with its yellow wall, slices through the residence to visually link the different levels together and to allow sunlight down to the main entry level.

The architecture's simplicity – exposed concrete walls and floors, galvanized metal siding, plasterboard infill walls and white laminate cabinetry – provide a neutral meeting of Japanese and Western influences that frame the location's view and weather.

Ryoichi Kojima - kodikodi architects

Sandwich House

Tokyo, Japan **Photographs:** Ayako Mizutani

Designed by Japanese architect and founder of Kodikodi Architecture, Ryoichi Kojima, this three story house stands in the highly compact neighborhood of Ota-Ku, the most populated of all of Tokyo's 23 wards. The challenge presented to the architects was to design a house for a couple and their child that would make the most spatially of its restricted site dimensions, while at the same time offering its inhabitants the desired levels of intimacy.

The client grew up in the Japanese countryside where most houses incorporate a backyard which is sandwiched between the main house and the shed. This arrangement effectively creates an outdoor space surrounded by a wall that lends the area surprisingly high levels of privacy. The architect took this idea and converted what would have been the backyard, i.e. the space between the two adjacent buildings, into the inside of the house.

In order to maintain interior privacy the architect placed two walls along the long site boundaries. These hold the 'backyard room' in place at first floor level producing the a floating space. This is used as a living area and has been located on the route from the dining zone to the house's more intimate sleeping quarters. The floating room thereby adopts the role of space divider and provides spatial variation. The structure has been clad in wooden boards, which, together with its sloping roof, produce an aesthetic similar to that of a garden shed.

On the top floor is a luxurious bathroom with an expansive wall-to-ceiling glazed opening that connects to an outdoor wooden terrace. The space has been designed to give those using the bathroom total privacy, yet when on the terrace excellent views can be had over the surrounding rooftops.

Since the wall space was severely restricted with regards to standard housing constructions, additional sunlight and ventilation were sought from the top of the house. A light well has been sliced right through the center of the property allowing air and light to enter and connecting all the different rooms and spaces. The suspended staircase penetrates this airy space exaggerating the perception of the size of the house for those inside. This also responds to the client's brief for a 'bright and fun house'.

Architecture:
Ryoichi Kojima - kodikodi architects

The challenge presented to the architects was to design a house for a couple and their child that would make the most spatially of its restricted site dimensions, while at the same time offering its inhabitants the desired levels of intimacy.

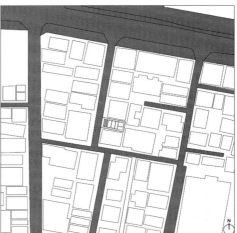

+3 floor plan

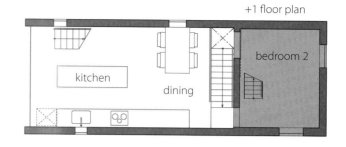

void

terrace

+1 floor plan

kitchen

dining

bedroom 2

+2 floor plan

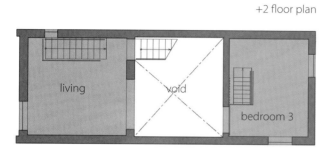

living

void

bedroom 3

Ground floor plan

garage

storage

bedroom 1

A floating living room has been 'jammed' between the two side walls of the house. This space recalls the backyard sheds from the Japanese countryside, where the client grew up.

Cross section

living

bathroom

bedroom 3

kitchen   dining

bedroom 2

garage

bedroom 1

Light and ventilation come from a shaft sliced through the middle of the structure. This increases the sense of size of the interior and incorporates a dramatic staircase, which serves to connect the entire house practically and visually.